Stop Blaming, Start Loving!

Stop Blaming, Start Loving!

A SOLUTION-ORIENTED APPROACH TO IMPROVING YOUR RELATIONSHIP

Bill O'Hanlon
and
Pat Hudson

W.W. NORTON & COMPANY
NEW YORK / LONDON

First published as a Norton paperback 1996

Originally published under the title *Love Is a Verb*

The text of this book is composed in 11/13 Bembo
with the display set in Poster Bodoni and Futura Book.
Composition and manufacturing by the Haddon Craftsmen, Inc.
Book design by JAM DESIGN

Library of Congress Cataloging-in-Publication Data

O'Hanlon, William Hudson.
Stop blaming, start loving! : a solution-oriented approach to
improving your relationship / Bill O'Hanlon and Pat Hudson.
        p.   cm.
Paperback ed. of: Love is a verb. 1995
Includes index.
ISBN 0-393-31461-8 (pbk.)
1. Man-woman relationships.   I. Hudson, Patricia O'Hanlon.
II. O'Hanlon, William Hudson. Love is a verb.   III. Title.
HQ801.O35   1996
306.7—dc20   96-16698
CIP

W. W. Norton & Company, Inc., 500 Fifth Avenue, New York, N.Y. 10110
W. W. Norton & Company Ltd., 10 Coptic Street, London WC1A 1PU

1 2 3 4 5 6 7 8 9 0

Contents

Acknowledgments

Thanks:

To Lofton Hudson, for the title, all the dinners, and the support.

To Mary Neumann, who knows that friendship is a verb.

To Carolyn Shulo, who makes sure Bill has his feet on the ground while he has his head in the clouds.

To Rhonda Applegarth, mutual admiration society member and air traffic controller for Pat and Bill's Dreamworld Airlines; we look forward to getting acknowledged in her first book.

To the many readers who helped make this book readable, especially Sandy Beadle, Marilyn Bronzi, Linda Hutton, Bonnie Marsden, Michael O'Brien, Kent Osborne, Gary Schultheis, and Lynn Skunta.

To our agent, Jim Levine, who encouraged and coached us in getting this whole project focused and published.

To our editor, Susan Barrows Munro, for helping us make the book more accessible.

To Margaret O. Ryan, our personal book doctor—we appreciate your hard work.

Stop Blaming, Start Loving!

1

THE CODEPENDENT CINDERELLA WHO LOVES A MAN WHO HATES WOMEN TOO MUCH

Analysis Doesn't Solve Relationship Problems and Can Even Make Them Worse

Once upon a time, Pat was at a party talking to a woman she had just met. When the woman found out that Pat was a psychologist, she began to tell Pat about her unhappy marriage. She said she was an adult child of an alcoholic who loved too much and was married to one of those men who hates women. It was clear the woman was very well read in the self-help arena. She knew everything there was to know about what was wrong with herself, her husband, and their relationship. Pat told the woman that she was thinking of writing a book entitled *Women Who Read Too Much*. The woman laughed and said she would probably read that one, too! Despite this woman's ongoing efforts to understand herself, however, she was not yet living happily ever after.

When things go wrong in our relationships, the first thing most of us do is try to find the problem by *analyzing* the relationship, our partner, and/or ourselves. Self-help books provide a variety of possible explanations. There is *The Dance Away Lover, Women Who Love Too Much, Men Who Hate Women, Adult Children of Alcoholics,*

Men's Fear of Intimacy, Codependent No More, and so on. You simply need to decide which particular psychological problem you or your spouse/partner has (we will use these terms interchangeably to refer to people in any romantic/sexual relationship, heterosexual or homosexual). We think that the "diagnoses" offered by these self-help books are really *problems* masquerading as solutions.

It's a bit like diets. Each year another diet program makes its debut. Dieters think they've finally found the *real* cause for their weight problem and the program that will finally work. For a few weeks or months they are enthusiastic (or maybe only a few *days,* if they've already tried a number of these programs). Then, when the program stops working, dieters slump into disillusionment. Perhaps criticisms of the program begin to appear in the media. For one reason or another the program falls by the wayside, only to be followed by yet another miracle diet program as the cycle continues. Just like the diet fads, psychological explanations of our innermost workings spring up all around us. We seem to have fallen prey to the "syndrome syndrome." Each year, a new crop of books is published hailing the discovery of a new syndrome *(The Peter Pan Syndrome, The Cinderella Complex)* that purportedly explains why your relationship is screwed up. Unfortunately, in relationships, as in dieting, having a good explanation for why things *aren't* going well is usually not very helpful. Why? Because having a good explanation, by itself, doesn't change anything.

The Solution-Oriented Relationship

This book is about a different approach to solving relationship problems. It comes from a new method of psychotherapy called solution-oriented therapy (Bill was one of the originators). Traditional therapeutic views focus on personality flaws and deficits of people who are having problems. Solution-oriented therapy focuses on people's strengths and inner resources, bypasses a lot of analysis, and gives people concrete ways of changing their *actions* and their *points of view.*

Change rarely occurs just as a result of getting in touch with your feelings, as traditional therapeutic approaches suggest. In fact, most of the people we see in marriage counseling are all too aware of how discouraged and angry they feel. After many years of helping couples solve their problems, we've discovered that *actions* offer keys to solutions. That is why we call this book *Stop Blaming, Start Loving!* Verbs are action words. We focus on actions as keys to effective communication and change.

Couples develop patterns of actions. You will learn how to identify and interrupt those unworkable patterns that cause recurring conflicts in your relationship. We will also help you to identify and use solution patterns from the past—actions that have worked for you before but that you may have overlooked as potential solutions for your current problems. We will show you how you can change your relationship by changing how you view things—your interpretation or point of view. Changing your point of view can lift you out of the rut you are stuck in and give you the power to make a difference in your relationship.

Translating problems and goals into actions is basic to this approach. By clearly identifying what you want to change in your relationship and finding out specifically what changes your partner would like, you will not only improve your relationship but also avoid blame and misunderstandings.

It Only Takes One to Stop the Tango

Most of us get discouraged when it seems that our partner is not willing to change or to work on the relationship. Fortunately, we have found that one person can change a two-person relationship by changing his or her part of the pattern or "the dance" of their interactions. We will give you easy, concrete methods for bringing about change in your relationship, even when it seems as if your partner does not want to cooperate in making those changes.

Focus on the Present and Future, Not the Past

Couples often get bogged down in their interactions because they try to analyze the past to identify what went wrong and who is to blame. Couples' arguments often go back to ancient mistakes, hurts, and resentments. It is important to acknowledge the past but then to focus on present and future goals. We will help you clarify what's not working for you in your current relationship and then show you the means to create a better future for yourself and your spouse.

Solution-oriented therapy is goal-oriented. Rather than looking for explanations in the past or focusing on what you *don't want*, we focus on helping you achieve what you *do want* as quickly and directly as possible.

KEY POINTS: SOLUTION-ORIENTED RELATIONSHIP

♥ To change your relationship, stop trying to analyze or change your or your partner's personality. Focus instead on changing actions, patterns, and points of view.

♥ Focus on the present, the future, and your goals rather than on the past.

♥ Remember that one person can change a two-person relationship.

What Psychologists Don't Want Us to Tell You

The guild of psychologists has a secret they don't publicize very much: *Nobody knows why we do the things we do.*

There are many competing theories about why we do what we do, but no general consensus as to which theory is right. Behaviorists say we do what we do because of rewards for certain behaviors. Genetically-oriented theorists claim that what we do is strongly influenced, if not determined, by our ancestry—what our parents passed on to us in their genes. Freudians believe our current behavior patterns are the product of early childhood experiences. And so on. So far, no theorist has been able to convince the other theorists that he or she has *the* answer. Probably they are all right, to some degree. Our behavior is probably not *caused* by any one factor but influenced by many: family background, socialization, present environment, early childhood experiences, what we eat, and more.

Bill was doing marriage counseling with a woman, Marj, and asked her, "What would you like your husband to do differently in your relationship?" She responded, "Well, he was raised in a family of five boys." Bill wondered how that was an answer to his question, until she explained that she knew it wasn't possible for her husband to give her what she needed. Being raised in a family of five boys had left him impaired, she had decided. She wanted him to be more physically affectionate—to hold her hand and put his arm around her from time to time. Marj had read somewhere that men, in general, are not very good at expressing affection physically, and especially if they were raised in families in which little touching occurred. She believed that her husband was incapable of doing what she wanted him to do. But Bill did not believe that Marj's husband had a muscle impairment that prevented him from reaching out and touching her. His arm still worked. In fact, when questioned more closely, Marj revealed that her husband had touched her more when they first dated and for a time after they married. As it turned out, it was not that difficult to get him to touch her more. Her explanation of his behavior had kept her from asking for what she wanted.

When things aren't going well in our relationships, we often develop explanations about what is wrong. We may become certain we know why we are having this problem: *he* came from a family of five boys, or *she* is just like her mother (or maybe worse, like *your* mother), or *he* has a fear of intimacy, or *she* has low self-esteem. Theorizing about the cause of your partner's behavior rarely solves the difficulty or creates a happier marriage.

In this book we are going to do our best to convince you that diagnosing yourself, your spouse, or the relationship is usually part of the problem, not the solution. We will offer an alternative for improving your relationship. This new course of action does not require experts to tell you the do's and don't of relationships. You can be your own expert. The tools for enhancing your relationship are already in your hands. It's just that nobody ever told you how to use them.

KEY POINTS: ACTIONS VERSUS EXPLANATIONS

♥ Nobody knows why we do the things we do (although there are many people who are convinced they do know).

♥ In relationships, explanations rarely solve problems.

♥ You can be your own expert. You have the ability to change your relationships.

Lost in Storyland

Each of us has our own point of view about things that happen in our relationships. We call these explanations *stories* to emphasize the fact that our points of view are not The Truth. Facts are different from stories. Facts are things we can all agree upon, what we can all verify with our senses. Stories involve opinions, interpretations, theories, and explanations. Facts are the "what"; stories are the "why."

We each use stories to explain what happens in our relationships. When there are problems or when people disagree, it often becomes a matter of "dueling stories." Whose story is right and whose is wrong? Neither. Both are explanations that cannot be proved either right or wrong.

> *Jim frequently bought Sherry gifts—flowers, candy, compact discs, concert tickets, and other things he thought she wanted. Sherry, however, had seen her father bring her mother gifts in an attempt to make up for all the times he was away from home. She had seen her mother become furious when her father failed to return home on schedule or when he missed another school play, only to be placated by the presentation a new coat or a car. Sherry viewed Jim's gifts as bribes, not as expressions of affection. She felt manipulated. Jim started to get the idea that Sherry was cold and angry, that there was something psychologically wrong with her, since she obviously couldn't appreciate his tokens of love.*

Most of us are caught up in the stories we believe about ourselves, other people, and our relationships; we have forgotten that these stories *are* stories and that *we* made them up. We are convinced that our stories contain The Truth and we often try to convince others of this "fact" (it's not a fact, only a viewpoint). We get into arguments about who is right or wrong. Is it a gift or a bribe?

In a courtroom, perhaps it is useful to decide who is right or wrong, but in your relationship, no matter which of you wins or loses the right/wrong battle, the relationship usually loses.

KEY POINTS: STORYLAND

♥ Stories are our interpretation and explanation of our experience.

♥ Stories are neither right nor wrong.

♥ Our stories do not reflect The Truth, only our perception of our personal truth.

♥ With dueling stories, the relationship loses, no matter who wins.

Stories That Hinder Relationships

Not all stories are created equal. When we get into difficulties, we typically develop stories that do not enhance our relationships. Out of frustration, anger or hurt, we come up with stories that hurt and blame. "You just want to control me." "You're just like your mother." "You care for your family more than you care for me." "You're selfish." We have identified three types of stories that hinder relationships by discouraging one or both partners: stories that *blame,* stories that *invalidate,* and stories that *eliminate possibilities.*

Blaming Stories

Some stories are blaming. Blame involves attributing bad intentions or bad traits to our partners. Blame also includes the accusation, *"You* are the problem."

*One couple we worked with, Robin and Kieran, were mak-
ing progress in marriage counseling, until Kieran came across an
article that he thought described Robin's problem exactly. She
was "obsessive-compulsive," he decided. He refused to make
any more changes as he was now convinced the cause of their
entire marriage problem was her personality disorder. Unfortunately, she did not agree. They were stuck. He thought the
problem was all her fault and she blamed him for not being willing to work on the marriage anymore. They may have each been
right, but it didn't help them change!*

People who feel blamed for the problems in their marriages often
become defensive and attack their partners back: "I wouldn't have
a problem if it weren't for you!" Or they decide that if they can't
get what they want, they'll at least make the other person hurt like
they're hurting. The relationship becomes a war of retribution and
vengeance—spouses become sparring partners rather than loving
partners.

Invalidating Stories

Other stories are invalidating because they give the message that
your partner cannot trust his or her perceptions or feelings. When
people feel invalidated, they start to lose confidence or may even
feel crazy. One of our favorite tales of attempted invalidation comes
from a book about affairs, *Private Lies,* written by our friend Frank
Pittman. Frank tells of a man who was followed to his lover's house
and was caught naked in the bedroom closet by his irate wife.
When she opened the closet door and saw him standing there, he
said compellingly, "You are hallucinating. I'm not really here. You
are imagining all this." She didn't fall for his ploy, but it was a
memorable attempt to get her to doubt her own perceptions.

Of course, in your relationship, invalidation probably occurs in
far more subtle ways. Maybe your partner says to you, "Why are
you so sensitive?" when you tell him your feelings were hurt when

he didn't introduce you to his boss at the Christmas party. Another subtle undercut: "You're not really angry at me. You haven't grieved for your father and you're taking it out on me and everyone else." Any statement that undermines your confidence in your experience and perceptions is a statement of invalidation.

Stories That Eliminate Possibilities for Change

Remember that your stories are not The Truth. Be careful of getting stuck with stories that convince you that change is impossible. Thinking that your partner can't or won't change is so discouraging you may even decide to end the relationship. We're not suggesting that you become unrealistically optimistic—only that you avoid prematurely giving up on your relationship because you believe your discouraging stories rather than experimenting to find out whether change is possible.

Pat saw a woman in counseling who was seriously considering ending her marriage. The problem, as Judy saw it, was that her husband, Tim, was a "wimp." He couldn't tolerate any conflict or negative emotions. He would leave the room if they started to have a disagreement or if she got upset. Judy worked in the evenings in a hospital and, if they had a disagreement before she went to work, Tim would proceed to clean the entire house while she was gone and make her a snack for her return. This behavior really annoyed her. (We know, many of our women readers are wondering what she was complaining about and probably want Tim's number.) The more frustrated Judy became, the harder Tim worked to smooth her feathers. But she wanted someone who could go "toe-to-toe" with her—she wanted a "man," not a "wimp." She had come to the conclusion that he would never change: he was born a wimp and he would die a wimp, and so she would never have the kind of relationship she wanted. A divorce seemed the only solution.

Our view was that this guy could change. Judy's story about him was not all there was to him. But she had become so convinced of the truth of her story that she almost divorced him. (We're going to make you wait for, as Paul Harvey says, "the rest of the story," until Chapter 3. How's that for keeping your attention?)

In *The Phantom Tollbooth,* a perennial favorite children's book around our house, some travelers find themselves unexpectedly jumping to the Island of Conclusions when they make statements for which they have no evidence. It is very easy to get to the island, but very difficult to return from that rather crowded place. It's the same in relationships. Once you make up your mind that your spouse *is* a certain way, the tendency is to go about gathering proof of your conclusion, making it very difficult to see any evidence to the contrary.

Another sure-fire way of eliminating possibilities is by pigeon-holing your partner. When things aren't working, one of the first things you may find yourself doing is searching for a label to explain your partner's frustrating or perplexing behavior. We call this process of labeling *hardening of the categories.* You stop seeing your partner as a person and start seeing him or her only in terms of your story, which relegates your partner to a category—perhaps as codependent, or as an adult child of an alcoholic, or commitment phobic. These negative labels stick like crazy glue, yet for all their tenacity, they do not help you solve the problem.

In medicine, labels can help us to identify the problem. If your blood pressure is consistently high, then you are "hypertensive." The label leads to some action that might solve the problem. In relationships, however, labels often not only don't lead to solutions, but become the problem. Psychology has given us many sophisticated-sounding labels that have the ring of scientific truth to them. These labels, however, are just stories. Getting home late used to be irresponsible; now it's "passive-aggressive." Caring about your mate use to be an ideal; now it can get you labeled "codependent." Life and relationships are becoming "medicalized" so that everyday difficulties have become full-fledged diseases.

Labels overlook the complexity of human behavior and reduce it to oversimplistic generalizations. After all, he is not *always* selfish; she does not *always* control things.

One night while walking around downtown, Bill and I ran into someone we both recognized but couldn't place at first. Finally, I realized she was our child's former pre-school teacher. I said, "Hi, Laurie. It's strange to see you here in another context. I guess you do have a life outside of pre-school." Laurie laughed and said that yes, she did have a life. Bill was happy that I had spoken first, since he was about to call the woman *Miss* Laurie. The point is that we tend to see people in one dimension. We forget that there are other sides to them. Most of the time this isn't much of a problem, but when it happens in a relationship, the consequences can be serious.

Labels are likely to upset the people to whom they are assigned, even if they agree with the label (which they usually don't). If someone told you that you were lazy, would that inspire you to do more? Probably not. Since it is impossible to know The Truth, we suggest you view your labels, if you have to have them, as hypotheses, not as proven facts. Fortunately, people do not come with tags that say, "Do not remove this label under penalty of law."

KEY POINTS: DIFFERENT KINDS OF STORIES

♥ Not all stories are created equal; some stories will help your relationship while others will harm it.

♥ There are three problematic kinds of stories that blame, invalidate, or eliminate possibilities for change.

Stop Blaming, Start Loving!

At the beginning of this chapter we said that analysis does not usually solve relationship problems. Why not? Because if there are conflicts in your relationship, your analysis involves stories that either blame or invalidate your partner, or that eliminate possibilities that your partner can change. Unfortunately, many self-help books on relationships actually advocate one of these problematic types of stories and therefore may worsen your conflicts.

Stop Blaming, Start Loving! offers two alternatives to these relationship-poisoning stories. The first, covered in detail in Chapter 2, asks you to describe, rather than theorize about, what is happening in your relationship. The second, detailed in Chapter 3, encourages you to be creative and start experimenting instead of drawing discouraging conclusions about yourself, your partner, and your relationship. The rest of the book applies these solution-oriented methods to common concerns in relationships: developing and enhancing intimacy, getting over past hurts, solving sexual problems, creating mutually satisfying sex, and sustaining the feelings of love and connection.

HOW TO STOP ANALYZING YOUR
RELATIONSHIP AND START MAKING IT GREAT

Becoming Your Own Relationship Expert

This chapter gives the basics of our simple method for resolving misunderstandings and getting more of what you want in relationships—communicating about actions you do not like and asking for actions you would like. This works much better than talking about theories, labels, or generalizations. You'll learn how to become your own relationship expert rather than relying on others to provide the formulas and theories you think you need but don't.

In order to make an important point about relationships, we are going to take a little journey back through evolution. (If you don't believe in the theory of evolution, that's okay—just consider this a metaphor.) Single-celled organisms such as amoebas don't have much freedom of choice. They react to their environments in predictable ways. You poke them ("Yow!") and they move away from you ("Danger, danger! Leave this vicinity immediately!"). You put some food near them ("Yum, that looks good and I've got the munchies") and they go towards it ("We amoebas only go around once in this swamp and we go for all the gusto we can get"). In other words, stimulate them and you can predict how they will respond.

As organisms become more complex, however, they have more freedom to choose how they respond. A more complex organism might have some sensor parts that specialize in scoping out the environment. If anything significant is detected, these sensor parts decide whether or not to pass the news on to the main body. So there is one choice. If the sensor parts decide to pass on the information ("Hey, dude, this could be significant, check it out!"), the organism can still decide whether or not to act on the information. By the time we get to dogs, behaviors become less and less predictable. If you pet a dog, you might get licked or you might get bitten. And by the time we climb the evolutionary ladder to humans, there are scads of choices. We're made up of billions of those amoeba-like cells, each making choices and decisions, gathering, filtering, and passing on information. What we do with that information is up to us.

Some people, though, continue to behave as though they were amoebas: In comes the stimulus, out comes the predictable response. Despite what you may have been taught to believe, you always have choices about your actions. Your past, your personality, the family you grew up in, your feelings, and other factors not withstanding, you can still choose to do something differently. If something upsets you, you can yell, pout, write a letter, leave the scene, go for a walk, or punch a wall. You have choices. As pop singer Bonnie Raitt says in the John Hiatt song, "We can choose, you know, we ain't no amoebas."

This chapter is based on a simple idea: it is easier for human beings to change their actions than their feelings or their personal characteristics. When there is a problem in a relationship, talking about actions and changing actions work better than trying to change the inside stuff. We'll give other reasons in the following sections, but for now we are simply suggesting that changing actions is easier, so why not take the path of least resistance?

Acknowledgment: Ten-four, Good Buddy

Problems we see in relationships often arise from something that is easy to solve. For example, couples get stuck arguing about who is right or wrong. Sometimes, of course, there is a right and wrong side to an argument, but most of the time partners fight because they have confused their own experience and perceptions with The Truth. The way each of us perceives, interprets, and feels in a given situation can be thought of as *personal reality,* and what we can actually verify, because we and others can see, hear, or touch it, can be thought of as *shared reality.* Getting your personal reality confused with the shared reality leads to problems. We'll give you ways to separate these two in the following sections. First, we want to make another suggestion: *avoid trying to change or correct your partner's personal reality.* If you try, she is likely to have one of two responses: either she will defend herself or she will withdraw from you (the old fight-or-flight syndrome).

Instead, we recommend simply *acknowledging* your partner's personal reality—feelings, perceptions, and interpretations. That doesn't mean agreeing with him. Just let him know the message was received. It's a bit like using a citizen's band (CB) radio. If you put out a call on the CB radio, respondents acknowledge that they have received your message by saying "Ten-four." They usually add "good buddy" for the homey touch. "Ten-four" is CB talk for, "Your message got through without a lot of static." Simply repeating back what your partner says usually gives the ten-four acknowledgment.

Your spouse may have sent a message that you don't like or don't agree with, and you might want to let her know that, but first you have to let her know that you received her message.

James and Erin were stuck in a fighting rut. They had been married two years and Erin's repeated complaint was that James did not treat her the way he used to. Whenever she would try to express this, James would immediately come back with, "No, I treat you better. I married you. I support us. I gave you my name." In breaking out of this rut, the first step was for James to slow things down long enough to say something like, "You feel that I've treated you differently since we got married." When he did this, the change in Erin was visible. She was so relieved to hear James acknowledge how she experienced their relationship.

Sometimes your partner is just asking for some acknowledgment—not agreement, not compliance, just *acknowledgment*. He or she wants to be heard and understood. Many conflicts would be avoided if each partner just took the time to acknowledge the other's feelings and points of view.

KEY POINTS: ACKNOWLEDGING YOUR PARTNER'S PERSONAL REALITY

♥ You can acknowledge by repeating back to your partner what he or she has just said in similar words to show you have heard and understood. Examples: "You were upset when I was late," or "You don't think I do anything around the house."

♥ You don't have to agree with your partner, but be careful not to invalidate him or her by saying things like, "That's crazy!" or "You are so wrong about that," or "Why are you so sensitive?" Remember, you are only acknowledging your partner's personal reality, not conceding that he or she has The Truth.

♥ Don't try to change your partner's inner qualities or experiences. For now, just acknowledge.

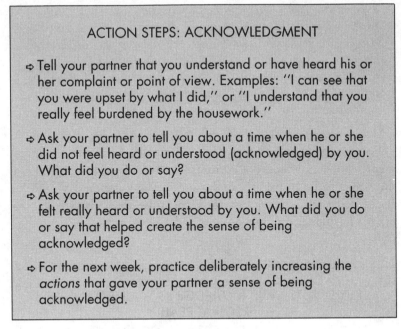

ACTION STEPS: ACKNOWLEDGMENT

⇨ Tell your partner that you understand or have heard his or her complaint or point of view. Examples: "I can see that you were upset by what I did," or "I understand that you really feel burdened by the housework."

⇨ Ask your partner to tell you about a time when he or she did not feel heard or understood (acknowledged) by you. What did you do or say?

⇨ Ask your partner to tell you about a time when he or she felt really heard or understood by you. What did you do or say that helped create the sense of being acknowledged?

⇨ For the next week, practice deliberately increasing the *actions* that gave your partner a sense of being acknowledged.

If acknowledging your partner's personal reality alone doesn't resolve the conflict, it's time to move into communicating in a new way that can solve problems without blaming, invalidating, or eliminating possibilities. We call this way of communicating "videotalk."

From Storyland to Videoland

We call this way of communicating *videotalk* because with it you describe what you want or don't want in terms of what you would see or hear on a videotape, avoiding adding any stories and interpretations. Instead of talking about your partner changing his or her inner qualities, in videotalk you talk about his or her actions.

Using videotalk to describe specific actions when communicating about conflicts is particularly helpful for clearing up misunderstandings. When couples are in conflict, misunderstandings and misinterpretations abound, typically sprinkled with stories that blame, invalidate, and eliminate possibilities, all of which poison the relationship. So we offer videotalk as an antidote to relationship poison. Our experience has shown that many couples can solve their problems quickly and easily with this method.

A couple who came for marriage counseling was on the verge of divorce. Milton was a recovering alcoholic who had stopped drinking about a year before. Kristina had expected him to change once he was sober. Now she had concluded that alcoholism had not been the problem; rather, Milton was cold and selfish as a person. He didn't care about anybody but himself. "Instead of drinking all the time," Kristina said with disgust, "now he works all the time or goes to AA meetings every night of the week. He never spends any time with me and our child." She had finally become so desperate that she had told him the night before this session that she was planning to seek a divorce. Milton agreed that he had been self-absorbed, both during his drinking years and since he'd been sober. But he contended that he could change. He vowed that if she would delay the divorce action, he would mend his ways. She agreed to give him a chance.

When they returned for another appointment two weeks later, however, they were both discouraged. He thought he had really gone out of his way to change his behavior for her and their family, but she didn't see any change. We asked Milton what he had done to show Kristina that he wasn't cold, selfish, and self-absorbed. "A lot," he told us, "but she didn't notice." "Give us one example," we suggested. "Well, yesterday, she came home from work with a bag of groceries in her arms. I put down the paper I was reading and met her at the front door, took the groceries from her, unpacked them, and put them away in the cupboards and refrigerator. I also cooked the vegetable for dinner that night."

We thought this effort deserved some credit, but she was quick to correct us. *"I could hire an assistant if I wanted help with the groceries and the cooking. I want a husband! I want someone who cares about me, who talks to me, listens to me."*

After some discussion, we asked Kristina to teach us and her husband what her husband could have done that would have looked like loving and caring behavior to her yesterday. She taught us that all she really wanted was for Milton to ask her how her day was each night after work and to listen attentively to her for fifteen minutes. She said that, night after night, he would rant and rave for an hour or so about his day and his troubles, but would never ask her how her day had been. She said he had asked her once, several years before, how her day had been. She happened to have had a terrible time that day and spent the next thirty minutes telling him about it. He never asked again, she said. He didn't think he never asked, but agreed to listen to her talk about her day for fifteen minutes each night (she gave him the weekends off) for the next two weeks. Kristina was skeptical that he would be able to do it, but he came through. That didn't resolve all their marriage problems, of course, but it gave her the sense that he could change and so she stuck around to work out the rest of their problems.

All Generalizations Are False (Including This One)

A common source of misunderstanding and conflict comes from using global generalizations to express complaints. Problems are easier to handle when they are stated in specific terms ("I'd like you to help me with the yard work for one hour on Saturday") rather than as global observations ("You never do any work around here!"). Global talk lends itself to misunderstandings because each partner tends to translate the general statements into different specifics.

> *During a divorce mediation session, we had reached an agreement that was painstakingly crafted. The agreement incorporated all the concerns of both parties and, in addition, contained renegotiation clauses in case of trouble. We had the impression that both partners could live with the agreement. But when we asked the couple how they felt about the agreement, the woman said vehemently, "Bullshit, bullshit, bullshit!" After a moment of stunned silence, Pat ventured, "Could you . . . be a little more specific?" Everyone broke up laughing and we continued the negotiation process.*

Couples commonly communicate in this way, using global words or phrases like *always, never, nobody, everybody, all the time, bullshit.*

If your husband has come home late *every* night since you've been married, then the generalization, "You are always late," is valid. Since we rarely have such precise knowledge, these broad statements are almost always inaccurate. A favorite generalization around our house is, "Nobody but me cares about this house!" which Pat once said in disgust while looking around at the mess. Now whenever I or one of the kids is doing some household cleanup, you can hear one of us exclaim, much to Pat's chagrin, "Nobody cares about this house but me!"

People often feel overwhelmed by negative generalizations that seem as if they are embedded in granite, never to be altered. Don't take your stories for granite (sorry, we couldn't resist). Sometimes when we are doing therapy with couples, we wish we had one of those buzzers from television game shows that goes off when the answer is wrong. We would buzz it whenever one of the partners uses a generalization. "She's *always* late!" *(Buzz!)* "He *never* wants to go out." *(Buzz!)*

KEY POINTS: GENERALIZATIONS

♥ Generalizations can easily lead to misunderstandings and discouragement.

♥ Generalizations make change seem as impossible as moving granite.

The Difference Between You and the Amazing Kreskin

Mind reading is another way people confuse their personal realities with shared reality. Perhaps you've seen the Amazing Kreskin. He's a professional mind reader. He stands on a stage and tells people he has never met what their birthdays are, significant facts about their lives, and even what dates or numbers they are concentrating on. The Amazing Kreskin is pretty good at reading people's minds, but the rest of us aren't.

There are two types of mind reading: (1) thinking you know what intention your partner has; and (2) thinking you know what your partner is thinking and feeling. When we attribute intentions to people, we are assuming that we can know what their motives are. For example, you might say, "My husband stays downstairs to watch television until late at night because he doesn't want to have sex with me." We can all agree with the "video" description, "He watches TV downstairs until midnight many nights, so we don't have much of a sexual relationship," but it would be hard to know with certainty *why* he stays downstairs and watches TV.

A woman complained that her husband spent all his time at work in order to avoid her. When he was confronted with this accusation, he denied it and supplied his own explanation: he stayed at work more than was necessary because he felt appreciated there.

When couples have conflicts, they don't usually give each other the benefit of a doubt. We came across a nice notion from a Lutheran catechism. The commentary says that the phrase "Love thy neighbor as thyself" means to give the most charitable interpretation to all that people do. When relationships are in trouble, couples tend to put the *least* charitable interpretation on all their partners do.

Of course, it is also possible to attribute positive motives to people's behavior. At a family birthday gathering at our house, our then two-year-old, Patrick, had gotten down from the dinner table and was walking around carrying a washcloth while the rest of us were finishing dinner. For no apparent reason, he swung the cloth around and whacked his grandmother on the arm. Rather than attributing negative intentions to her grandson, she said in a sweet voice, "Were you wanting Grandma's attention?"

The second form of mind reading is claiming to know what your partner is feeling or thinking. We often guess what people feel or think based on their actions or even their facial expressions. When Pat and I were dating, every once in a while Pat would ask me, "What's wrong?" To me, these seemed to be random inquiries. It turned out that Pat would ask this question whenever I sighed. To Pat, sighing meant that I was worried or bored or somehow upset. I learned to handle this by breaking into song and reminding Pat that "a kiss is just a kiss" and "a sigh is just a sigh."

Sometimes we think that *love* equals *psychic abilities*. We expect our partners to read our minds or know what we want without our telling them directly.

Although you may be able to teach others to do what you want in response to your nonverbal cues, at least some of the time people won't be able to guess what they are supposed to do. If you want your spouse to touch you when you're being quiet, you'd better tell him about that sometime when you're not being quiet.

Pat's parents celebrated their fiftieth wedding anniversary some years back. Her father was firmly against having a big party. Pat knew that her mother wanted one, so she asked her mother how she felt about not having a party. Her mother replied in her soft southern accent, "Oh, it's fine with me, dahlin', as long as he gives me a dozen yellow roses." Pat asked her mother if she had told Pat's father about the roses; her mother said she had not. Later Pat told this story to the children and one of them said, "You know, it sounds like Grandma is expecting Grandpa to read her mind and the problem is that it's illegible!"

We are not saying that you should only talk about facts, never telling your story. We are just saying that if you get the two confused, problems often result. We have found that sharing stories is not destructive when they are clearly acknowledged as stories and not as truths. For example, if you are not having sex as often as you used to, you might say: "I notice that we have not been making love as often as we used to. I was wondering if that was because we have too much to do? Or is it that you're bored with the same old partner?" Compare that with, "I know we're not making love because you're bored with me"—a here's-the-truth type of statement that immediately puts your partner on the defensive.

KEY POINTS: MIND READING

♥ Mind reading means that you think you know what is going on inside your partner without being told.

♥ There are two types of mind reading: (1) attributing intentions or motives to your partner; and (2) guessing what your partner is feeling, thinking, or experiencing.

♥ Don't expect your partner to be able to read your mind and know what you want, what you are thinking, or what seems like love to you.

Is Love Really Never Having to Say You're Sorry?

Another way couples confuse their personal realities with the shared reality is by using global terms, assuming that they have *the* definition of these generalities. As we mentioned earlier, you can tell if you are sticking with the facts if you make what we call *"X = X"* statements. For example: "love is love," "sex is sex," "helping with the dishes is helping with the dishes," "saying you're sorry is saying you're sorry." For most of us the notion of love and of many vague concepts that have multiple meanings is equal to something else *(X = Y)*. We believe that love equals things like having sex when we want it, having an exclusive sexual relationship, doing the housework, talking in certain voice tones and not others, and so on. Love equals a certain combination of actions which our partner does in relationship to us. Unfortunately, we rarely let our partner know what our definition of love is—what love looks like and sounds like to us. Or, for that matter, we haven't defined what "respect," "caring," "honesty," and other such general concepts equal in action-land. These unshared definitions of key emotions and characteristics are the source of some serious difficulties in relationships.

For *your* partner, love may be never having to say you're sorry. If *you* think love is saying you're sorry often, then you've got a problem.

> *One couple Pat worked with discovered that they had completely different ideas about giving and receiving love. Jamal was very romantic and believed that love was demonstrated by things like surprise picnics and candlelit dinners. His wife, Denise, thought that Jamal could show her love by helping with the housework, arranging to have the wallpaper hung in the family room, and cleaning his whiskers out of the bathroom sink after he shaved. Once they accepted that neither of them had the correct view of what love really is, each could begin to give love*

to the other in a way that he or she recognized. They later told Pat that this idea of teaching each other their different definitions of love had been so helpful to them that they had developed the habit of asking each other upon awakening each morning, "What can I do to show you my love today?"

Many other words we use in relationships have multiple meanings that can lead to misunderstandings: "independence," "dependency," "dependable," "attentive," "affectionate," "fair," "cooperative," "efficient," "helpful," and so on. If you hear words like these in your disagreements, try for the video descriptions. For example, your spouse might complain that he or she didn't feel respected. What does respect look like on a videotape? How do you know when you are or are not getting it?

What do you do if you *can't* describe the actions you don't want your partner to do? Sometimes your complaint may be something like a voice tone or a facial expression that you have difficulty describing, so you may need to point it out as it occurs.

You can avoid getting stuck in your stories by considering that the opposite of the way you think about some situation could also be valid. We call this the *or not* technique. To use it, simply add the phrase "or not" or its equivalent to pronouncements, like "people who love each other do not fight." Either they fight or they don't. "You're angry with me." Either you are angry or you're not. This can remind you to open your mind to the possibility that what you are thinking is *your* idea about the way it is and not necessarily *the* way it is.

There is no universal dictionary that can tell us what love or respect is, in an absolute sense. All we can know is that love is love and respect is respect. Asking for what you want is fine. Just keep in mind that your definitions of love and respect are made up, definitely in the land of stories. That doesn't make your definitions invalid; it just makes it essential for you to tell your partner what those words mean to you.

Action Complaints: From Kvetching to Communication

I personally think we developed language
because of our deep need to complain.
Lily Tomlin
Search for Signs of Intelligent Life
in the Universe

As we discussed in previous sections, most of us speak pretty generally and vaguely when communicating. We use words that can mean different things to different people. We think of these as "packaged words." It's as if UPS has delivered a package to your house, and on that package is a label. For example, the label on the box might be "passive-aggressive." You don't know what's in the box and what the label means until you open the box and examine the contents. So we ask, "What does passive-aggressive mean?" For one person the answer might be: "Passive-aggressive means that he tells me he'll be home at 6:00 for dinner and he doesn't come home until 7:30 and doesn't call." For another: "Passive-aggressive is when we have an argument and she doesn't say anything, but the next day she forgets to pick me up at work." Only by unpacking these packages can you and your partner uncover the specific action-contents inside.

When couples first seek our help, they mainly talk about what they *don't* like about each other. Their complaints not only reach back to the distant past (something that is very difficult to change) but also involve a great deal of blaming, mind-reading, and vague talk in the present. There is a wonderful Yiddish word that captures this kind of interaction—it's *kvetching*. Kvetching is a dreary kind of repetitive complaining, nagging, and whining. Most couples start their first session with us kvetching. We begin our work by helping them change their kvetching into *action complaints*—complaints that can make a difference. Action complaints clearly identify behaviors that elicit the disturbing response; generalities are avoided. Complaints expressed in vague terms, such as, "You're not being *nice* to me," are usually ineffective because they don't give your partner clear indications about what he or she is doing that irritates you. If you say instead, "I don't like it when you come into the house after work and go to the bedroom to change your clothes without greeting me," you are offering an effective action complaint. Your partner knows right away exactly what he or she is doing that you don't like.

When there is trouble in your relationship, you may not even notice what your spouse is doing that upsets you. You might just notice that you are not feeling loved or that you are feeling lonely or angry. It is natural to ask yourself, "why?" The difficulty can come in the next step, when you answer your own question. Deciding that your mate doesn't love you (your story) is unlikely to lead to positive change in the relationship. However, translating "not being loving" into actions (videotalk) can lead to change. Saying, "I feel criticized and unloved when you use phrases like, 'You're just like your mother'," identifies specific actions that you want your partner to change.

Rita complained that her husband, Rob, did not respect her. He disagreed with her conclusion, contending that he did respect her. When we asked her for a recent example of Rob's disrespect, Rita reported an incident at a party when she had given her political opinion and her husband had snorted. Rita had concluded that this indicated Rob's lack of respect for her political opinions and, perhaps, even her right to voice them. Rob confessed that he could not remember snorting on that occasion, but he admitted that he might have done it. He agreed not to make noises through his nose when she was expressing her views.

It is probably best to stick with the recent past and present when using action complaints. It is usually easier to recall specific details about an event that has just happened. If only one of you remembers a long-past event clearly, you can get sidetracked talking about whether or not your description of the past is accurate. If you limit your complaint to the recent past or present, you are more likely to focus on behaviors that can be changed in the near future, which increases the odds of getting results.

KEY POINTS: ACTION COMPLAINTS

♥ Make your complaint "video-clear," focusing on actions, words, facial expressions, gestures, and voice tones and volumes.

♥ Translate packaged words into specific descriptions and incidents.

♥ Avoid blaming, labeling, mind reading, and generalizing.

♥ Complain about actions, not personality traits, which are hard to change.

♥ Telling your partner your interpretation (story) about his or her actions is okay. Just remember to distinguish it from the facts (videotalk) and to realize that your partner probably has an entirely different story about the same situation.

♥ Digging up past hurts is not helpful; stay focused on recent events.

R-E-S-P-E-C-T, Find Out What It Means to Me: Action Requests

In the last section we talked about telling your spouse what you want him or her to stop doing or to change. Once you have expressed your complaint in this clear way, it is time to provide a road map of directions by letting your partner know what you would like him or her to do differently in the future. It's time to move from complaints to action requests. Often it is easy to move from the complaint to the request because you only need to think of what the opposite behavior would be. For example, if your complaint is that your partner does not look at you when you are talking, the obvious request would be for him or her to look at you when you are speaking.

What makes action requests different from the common way we ask for change is that the requestee knows what to do when the requester has finished speaking. Action requests involve: asking for specific actions; including as much detail as possible in terms of time, place, and behaviors so that the requestee can know exactly what is expected; and follow-up checkpoints. You might make a request that your partner "be nice," but we doubt that he or she would know what to do differently.

Frank complained that his wife Cheryl was closer to her woman friend than she was to him. Next, he needed to translate his desire for closeness into action requests: things he did not want Cheryl to do and things that he did want her to do. He asked that she not discuss certain topics with her friend, such as their sex life, and he asked that she tell him each day how she was feeling and, specifically, how she was feeling about him.

Cheryl had her own requests, too. Cheryl's friend treated her in a "positive" way. Cheryl needed to give Frank a video description of what positive treatment meant to her so that she would be willing to open up to him. To her this meant that Frank should make eye contact with her when she was talking, he should not jump in with suggestions about what she should do, and he should compliment her.

Asking for specific actions and then seeing your partner actually *do* those actions can inject new hope into a faltering relationship. Avoiding stories and making your request action clear are the essence of effective communication.

Marge had asked that Ralph give her a hug every night when he came home. Although he had given her hugs regularly as requested, Marge said that his hugs were perfunctory. He would just lightly squeeze her shoulder for a couple of seconds. We devised a remedial hug training session in which Marge taught Ralph that a hug meant both hands on the back with firm pressure, embracing for at least forty-five seconds. As an engineer, Ralph appreciated these precise guidelines.

What types of things should you be certain to include in your request? The first and most important, of course, is the video description. If you were to watch a videotape of your partner doing exactly what you want, what would the scenario look like? What actions would you see? What words would you be hearing?

Often, requests involve a time frame. For example, if your request is that your partner spend more time with you, you want to be certain to make that very specific. You could say, "I would like for us to go out to dinner alone every Thursday night."

Jane, a career woman, came into a session saying that her husband, Bob, recently retired from the Air Force, did not "give her any space." They were an attractive couple in their thirties who had been separated for a year. They came to therapy to "give it one last try," before making a decision to stay together or divorce. Jane clarified her request for "space," saying that she had no time to herself; she was either at work or with her husband. In the session Bob willingly agreed that she could have Thursday nights as her own. We asked Jane to specify whether or not that meant that they should have dinner together, or if one of them should leave the house. Jane decided she wanted to have post-dinner time in a certain part of the house by herself. Bob was welcome to stay or go, but if he stayed home, he should work in his shop in the garage. This time alone could be over by 10:30 P.M.

It may seem that going into such detail is excessive, but we have found that making your desires crystal clear is often the road out of difficulties. Sometimes requests include checkpoints to see if the plans made to fulfill the request are working. If you make an agreement to spend more time together, you might want to set a specific time on the first day of each month for mutual feedback.

We think of these requests as including what could be called the "criteria for satisfaction." What needs to happen for you to feel that your request was satisfied? For example, if you wanted to feel more loved, then your requests might include several behaviors that would have to happen before you truly felt loved: being asked about your day, touching in bed at night, making love twice a week, and receiving compliments.

Some people ask, "How do I know that this will work?" Our answer is that we are not guaranteeing that this will work, just suggesting that you give your partner clear guidelines for making a change. It is like an experiment. You ask the other person to try specific actions and you try specific actions as well and then see if the relationship can be what you want. Sometimes when the request doesn't lead to change, you'll find that you have made an assumption and have not clearly communicated. One time Pat and I had a conflict because she expected me home at "dinnertime" and, according to her, I was late. "I was not late!" I exclaimed in surprise. After a discussion, we found out that I assumed that dinnertime was 6:00 to 6:30 and she thought it was 5:30. So be sure you have been specific with all the aspects of your request.

Later we'll discuss what to do if your partner isn't cooperating or doesn't follow through on commitments to change, but here we are helping you make sure you have at least communicated clearly and specifically about what you want.

Another concern we hear is: "What about feelings? This approach seems so mechanical, so focused on behaviors. Isn't love a *feeling,* not a bunch of actions? Do you talk two like this to each other at home? Where's the heart stuff?" Of course, love involves feelings. And, no, we don't talk like this to each other *all the time* at home. We only use action complaints and requests to avoid misunderstandings and clear up conflicts. Love isn't only actions, but without actions and videotalk, you can't express it or teach your partner how you receive it.

KEY POINTS: ACTION REQUESTS

♥ Make requests as specific as possible about time frames and actions.

♥ Avoid vague words and stories (explanations and theories about why your partner has or hasn't done things) when making requests.

♥ If the requests do not work, re-phrase the request or see if there is a misunderstanding about the actions requested.

♥ Action requests involve communicating clearly to your partner about what actions constitute your "criteria of satisfaction" for fulfilling your request.

ACTION STEPS: ACTION REQUESTS

⇨ Ask your partner to fill in the blank in the following sentence. "I would like you to _____ [description of some action your partner would like you to do in the future] by _____ [fill in the date]."

⇨ Give your partner one request using action language. "I would like you to _____ [description of some action you would like your partner to do in the future] by _____ [fill in the date]."

Catching Your Partner Doing Something Right:
Meaningful Praise

It's a tried and true principle of behaviorism, business management, and parenting that it is much more effective to encourage actions that are already occurring than to try correcting actions that you want to eliminate. Lab experiments have shown that rats repeat behaviors that are rewarded. If it works on rats, why not try it with your partner? (Next chapter, we'll discuss a crucial difference between rats and human beings, but here we are using rats to make a point.)

When partners are in conflict, they usually forget to comment on what is going right in the relationship. If they do give feedback, it is often given in such vague ways that the other is not sure why he or she is being praised. Therefore, it's hit-and-miss as to whether the praise will work.

"Meaningful praise" remedies this randomness. Like action complaints and requests, meaningful praise involves giving specific details—videotalk. Instead of simply saying, "I felt really close to you this week," we recommend that you tell your partner what, specifically, he or she *did* that helped you develop that feeling of closeness. Bill has told me that he's willing to make changes in our relationship as long as I let him know what works for me. (Bill jokes that he is a slow learner, but trainable.) I invented a code phrase that I use anytime I spot Bill doing something right. I just say, "That's G.H.B., Bill." By now, Bill knows that G.H.B. stands for "Good Husband Behavior."

Diane and Joe began their second session saying that things were just as bad as ever. Pat asked, "Was that true for the whole two weeks or was there a time when things went better?" Diane said, "Things were wonderful for the first five days after our last session." Pat seized upon this opportunity to elicit details of what happened during those first five days. Diane said, "Joe was being my companion." Pat asked Joe if he knew what Diane meant by companionship. *Joe said that he had done a couple of things he thought might fit her definition of companionship: he had gone shopping with her and taken her dancing. Pat checked with Diane to be sure that Joe had correctly identified the companionship actions. He had. Pat emphasized two things: one, that Joe was capable of companionship actions; two, that if they could keep the ball rolling in that direction, things could improve fairly easily. To help accomplish this, Diane agreed to tell Joe when he was doing "good companionship" actions.*

Meaningful praise involves catching your partner doing something *right*. When things are not working, we usually become skilled at catching our partner messing up. To turn things around, just ask yourself, "What has my partner done this week that I liked or appreciated?" When you have identified what that or those things were, use videotalk to let him or her know.

For instance, one time I was sitting in the living room reading when Pat came by and, noticing it was turning dark, switched on the reading lamp. I looked up and told her how much I appreciated the thoughtful little things she did. That evening we were out to dinner with Pat's father, Lofton. We mentioned the lamp incident and how rarely married couples compliment one another. I said, "You know, though, Lofton. I'll bet if someone had turned on that light for you, you would have reached over and turned it off and said, 'Who made *you* my mother!' " Lofton laughed and admitted I was probably right about that. Remember, one person's definition of love and caring may be another person's definition of control and smothering. That's why you can't read that article in *Cosmo* telling you the "Ten Ways to Jump Start Your Husband" and be certain that those ways will work for you and your partner. The things that jump start someone else's partner may drain your partner's battery.

KEY POINTS: MEANINGFUL PRAISE

♥ Use videotalk to describe current or past actions you liked when your partner did them.

♥ Remember that there aren't any lists of "good husband or wife behavior," but with this model you and your partner can be the experts who teach each other what works.

ACTION STEPS: MEANINGFUL PRAISE

⇨ Catch your partner doing something that you appreciate once each day for the next week. Let him or her know about it as specifically and quickly as possible.

⇨ Write a love letter to your partner telling him or her about a time when you felt really close or loved. Be sure to include specific descriptions of what he or she did that led to your feelings.

Negotiated Agreements

What can you do if one partner wants some action the other is not willing to do? This section gives four simple methods for negotiating those seemingly irreconcilable conflicts to obtain win-win results: finding another action you can both agree upon, compromising, taking turns, and shelving the disagreement.

Find Another Action You Can Both Agree Upon

Dave and Laurie were at an impasse. They had attended our relationship seminar before coming to therapy. Dave had asked that Laurie be more adventuresome sexually. Laurie wanted to please Dave but he wanted her to take a leap she was not willing to make. To Dave, being "sexually adventuresome" meant having anal sex. Pat suggested they look at the category "more adventuresome about sex" and find what other actions they could agree upon. Laurie was modest; she would not usually wear anything from a Victoria's Secret catalog other than a sweatshirt. She decided that she would be willing to be more adventuresome sexually by wearing a teddy, a garter belt, and hose. While this didn't completely meet Dave's desires, it gave him the message that she cared about his sexual desires and was willing to try some different behaviors to spice things up.

Usually you can find another action that would fit into the general category of actions being requested; there are always other ways to show love, support, or unselfishness. If your spouse asks you to give up some activity you love—be it watching football, scoping out garage sales, or participating in self-help groups—find out what the underlying consideration is. If your partner objects to your being gone so often, change something else in your schedule and reserve time. Perhaps you can find a way to meet your partner's needs and still do other things you enjoy. We think of this way of resolving conflicts as moving back and forth between *general categories* and *specific actions* to find what would satisfy the person making the request and be agreeable to the other.

Bill travels out of town three times a month to train therapists. When we were first together, I wanted him to call every day when he was gone. He felt that was too much of a burden, as he often had a hectic schedule while on the road. To find some other way to meet my needs, he asked what my main concern was. I said that sometimes things came up, particularly with our children, and that I needed his input. The initial action requested was "call every day," but the real need was different: "be available if I need you." Bill offered a new action option by promising that he would always leave a telephone number where he could be reached, so that I could always contact him. He also agreed to call every other day when he was in the country and every three days when he was abroad. This became a non-issue after the birth of our last child. Then sleeping ten more minutes became more important to me than receiving a telephone call from Bill!

In this example, Bill was the one who was doing the changing. When both partners have to make some kind of change, it's time to compromise.

Compromise

The dictionary tells us that compromise involves both sides making concessions.

Jamie and Mandy found themselves constantly squabbling over meal preparation. They both had demanding jobs and, with a young child, they were both feeling overwhelmed with duties when they came through the door to their apartment at night. Jamie said that Mandy was the better cook, so preparing meals should be her domain. Mandy felt that, even if she were Julia Child, it should not fall on her shoulders to be the exclusive preparer of food. She wanted Jamie to do half the cooking. They were both hesitant to go out to eat very often because, first, it was expensive and, second, their three-year-old was not the ideal restaurant patron. Their usual discussions had involved talk about his being a "sexist" and her being "unreasonable." That hadn't gotten them far. After going around and around with this issue, they finally decided to split the difference. Jamie agreed to somehow muddle through the meal preparation two nights a

*week; Mandy agreed to do three nights; and they would do
take-out one night and find a family restaurant on a weekend
night. They split the difference—they compromised.*

So one way to handle what seems to be an unsolvable problem is
to split the difference between your two positions. Another way to
compromise is for each partner to decide to give up something he
or she wants in return for the other giving up something.

*Joleen and Marcus had begun to argue every night. She ac-
cused him of being a "workaholic," as he stayed at work from
early in the morning until late at night. Out of boredom and in
retaliation, she began going out to bars with her single girl-
friends. He thought going to the bars made it likely she would
have an affair and so he was angry when she continued to go
after he asked to stop. With our help, they struck a bargain. She
would stop going to the bars if he made it home by 8:00 P.M.
every night. He had to change his "workaholic" patterns and she
had to give up her "girls night out."*

Taking Turns

When partners are unwilling to meet halfway, then experimenting
with each partner's plan for a limited time may be the answer. For
example, couples typically fight over some aspect of parenting
sooner or later. Discipline, curfew, and school performance can all
provide fields for battle. Agreeing to experiment with doing things
one way or the other for a certain amount of time can help couples
resolve an impasse.

*Jean and Pete fought over whether spanking was acceptable as
a consequence for their four-year-old's challenging behavior.
Jean argued that their son became more violent when they used
spanking, and Pete said that being spanked had not hurt him and*

he felt it was good for the boy. Jean had become so upset about the issue and Pete's unwillingness to compromise that she told him she was seriously considering divorce. They agreed to try one month of using spanking as the means of discipline and one month of using only time-out as a consequence. Ultimately, they found that their son was less combative and more cooperative the month during which they used time-out, so Jean and Pete agreed to stick with the time-out method.

When Martin and Jill had begun their relationship, they lived in different cities. On the weekends they would get together and have sex, occasionally as many as ten times per weekend. After a couple years of a long-distance relationship, they decided to marry and live in the same city. As time went on, Jill became less interested in sex. As her fervor waned, Martin became increasingly desperate and obnoxious in his pursuit of her. He would rub up against her with an erect penis, look hurt, sigh a lot, and spend the evening dropping hints about what would happen later. This behavior annoyed Jill and only decreased the likelihood that she would have sex with him. They came to see Bill for therapy. Bill asked how often they each would like to have sex. Jill said she didn't even know anymore because she had become so turned off, but she thought two or three times a week might be nice. Martin preferred at least once a day. Bill suggested that Jill and Martin take turns. One week Jill would be in charge of the frequency of sex, guaranteeing Martin at least one sexual interaction in which he would have an orgasm (not necessarily intercourse). Martin would then have his week to be in charge of the frequency. When they came back a month later, Martin said, "I want all the weeks to be her weeks!" When Jill was in charge, she was able to discover her own rhythm of desire and enthusiasm for sex, and the genuineness of her response convinced Martin that quality, not quantity, mattered most.

Some dilemmas are easily resolved by taking turns, whereas other kinds of difficulties are not. What do you do when compromise, taking turns, and alternative actions are out of the question?

Shelve the Disagreement, But Don't Withdraw from the Relationship

If you have a conflict that cannot be resolved in the usual ways, you can agree to shelve it for a while without withdrawing from the relationship. For example, some of the most challenging conflicts in working with couples arise over disagreements about whether or not to have a baby. You can't find a compromise—there are no half babies. You can't try parenting out and see how you do. Your either are a parent or you are not.

> *John and Paula had agreed to have children when they married. He had two daughters from a previous marriage. She had not been married before and was now ready to start being a mother. John began to backpedal on the parenting idea. First, he said, he was deeply concerned about Paula's rages. He reported that, as they were driving down the highway having an argument about the baby decision, Paula had become so angry that she tried to kick the windshield out of the car. He wondered whether or not he should risk putting a child in such a volatile environment. Second, if the rages continued at this level, he was not so sure he could tolerate living with Paula at all. He was already a noncustodial parent and he did not want to have another child he could not be with on a daily basis.*
>
> *They came to see Bill in this conflict. His suggestion was that they work on their relationship and simply put aside the parenting issue for six months. Paula learned other ways to deal with her anger, so she stopped having rages. John did not immediately change his mind; however Paula decided that she would stay with John, even without having children, and put more emphasis on her career. Rather unexpectedly, a few months later, John announced that he was ready to have a child. They have since had a daughter and are both very happy with their lives.*

This story had a happy ending, but of course many people do end their marriages because of conflicts over having children and other nonnegotiable issues. Fortunately, most relationship issues lend themselves to other options and the first three strategies—finding other actions that will satisfy both partners, compromising, and taking turns—are usually very successful. If you have tried the things we've suggested in this chapter and they haven't helped or if your partner doesn't seem interested in changing, the next chapter tells you how to alter your relationship in another way.

3

THE DIFFERENCE BETWEEN A RUT AND
A GRAVE IS THE DIMENSIONS

Changing Unworkable Patterns

Communicating clearly and without blame and invalidation resolves many relationship problems, but not all of them. Our title, *Stop Blaming, Start Loving*, refers to the idea that people can get into good or bad action patterns in relationships. Again, instead of analyzing why the patterns are there or where they came from, we offer action tools to quickly change the patterns. These tools are simple to apply and are often fun and creative.

Sometimes we all get stuck in viewing people in very fixed ways. We think of them as set *things* rather than as changeable individuals. In this chapter, we offer a different way to think about people—as *patterns*. Patterns are easier to change than things. What we call "personality" is a shorthand way of saying that people act consistently over time. When people do have "personality changes," what actually changes are their habits of action.

Relationships also develop their own personalities. These relationship personalities are patterns of action, habits, that can be changed. In fact, we think that *relationship* personalities are easier to change than individual personalities, because relationship personalities develop later in life. Furthermore, it takes two people acting consistently to make a relationship personality. If either one of them changes, the relationship can (and most likely will) change.

Individual Patterns

We call patterns that are just yours "individual patterns." These individual patterns characterize your behavior no matter whether you are with one person or another. How do you identify your own individual pattern? Look at several relationships, several settings, and notice if people usually label you or complain about you in the same way. If you are in a relationship with one person and she calls you "possessive," then you become involved in another relationship and that person calls you possessive too, the consistency of the feedback suggests that the pattern you do is possessiveness. Not that you *are* possessive, but that you *do* possessiveness.

If the people at work, your spouse, and the person who fixes your car all complain that you are too much of a perfectionist, that repeated feedback indicates that you *do* a pattern of actions that people see as perfectionistic.

In Eastern philosophy, there is a notion that if you don't settle something in this life, you must be reborn into another life until you finish whatever is unfinished. This is called your "karma." (If you completely miss the lessons you are supposed to learn, you have to come back as a cockroach and work your way back up to a human being over several lifetimes. No fun!) The same could be said for relationships. If you have a pattern of behavior that you repeat from relationship to relationship, that can be thought of as your "relationship karma." If you don't settle the issue in the relationship you are in, it will pop up in the next one and the one after that, until you finally learn how to change or modify the pattern. We have all heard about patterns that people repeat throughout their relationships. Most of us know someone who grew up in a home in which one parent had a problem with alcohol who later married someone who had a problem with alcohol. (Of course, many people who grew up in such homes did not choose a spouse with alcohol problems—theories claiming that children of alcoholic parents will always marry an alcoholic are generalizations.) Now remember that this idea about relationship karma is just a story. We don't believe it is *true* for all people in all relationships, as some self-help writers would have you believe. We use it here only to make a point.

One of the clues to identifying your relationship karma is noticing if the same kind of pattern starts to develop in your relationship with very different kinds of people. I was amazed when Bill, who was very easygoing when we first met, became unusually irritable several years into our relationship. My first husband had been very cranky with me at times as well, so I jokingly suggested that it must be an acidic condition of my body that made the men I married irritable. Ultimately I realized that the way that I handled grumpiness increased it or inadvertently rewarded it. If my first husband said something critical, I would just try harder to please him and feel more and more alienated from him. When this pattern happened with Bill too, I decided to nip it in the bud. If Bill used a cranky voice tone with me I would immediately say, "Please don't use that voice tone with me." Bill responded well to these requests and I did not have to go through my old pattern of trying harder and harder to please someone who was using a critical, harsh voice tone and eventually not wanting to be around the critic.

Before I met Pat, I had a pattern of getting into struggles with partners over wanting to spend time alone, reading or just being by myself. Inevitably my partner would feel that I was avoiding or rejecting her. After several relationships in which this same problem arose, I started to wonder whether I was doing anything to contribute to it (remember, I'm a slow learner, but trainable—it only took me four or five relationships to begin to wonder about this). As I thought about my past relationships, I noticed that I had spent most of my time attending to my partner at the beginning, when our energy was intense. After that initial focus, I would miss reading and spending time by myself, but would feel a little bad about withdrawing. So I would find excuses to get away or hide the fact that I had been reading. My partners would quickly respond to these actions by becoming upset and critical. I would get defensive and withdraw even more to sneak in my reading. On and on it went until it became a real problem pattern. By the time I met Pat, I had discovered that it was important to take some time early in the relationship to read, even if my natural inclination was to spend all my time with Pat. That chronic problem—my relationship karma—hasn't been an issue in our relationship. (Perhaps, I won't have to come back as a cockroach in my next life since I have mastered this major life lesson!)

Relationship Patterns

Social scientists have noted that actions (behaviors) occur in settings (contexts) and that it is difficult to study behavior independent of the context that is strongly influencing it. We fall into patterns with people when our response to them creates a context for them to do the next part of the pattern. If your partner is angry with you and you respond to the accusations by saying, "That's a good point," you have created a very different context than if you launched into defending the opposite point of view. As we promised earlier, let us tell you what happened to the guy whose wife thought he was a wimp and would never change.

When Tim, the husband, discovered that his wife, Judy, had scheduled an appointment to meet Pat, he telephoned Pat and told her he'd do anything *to save the relationship.* When Pat saw Judy, she realized that Judy was pretty serious about getting a divorce. Pat suggested that Judy should at least give marriage counseling a try before giving up entirely. She agreed and Pat got permission to talk to Tim about what they had discussed. When he telephoned, Pat had only a few minutes between appointments to speak with him. She told Tim that Judy had stereotyped him as a wimp. Tim said he knew that, but he felt helpless to do anything about it. Pat told Tim that since their joint session was two weeks away, he should start to experiment with acting in ways that didn't fit the stereotype of wimp—anything that was out of character for him but was not dangerous or unethical.

When they came in their joint session two weeks later, they told Pat a surprising story. One afternoon they sat down to have a discussion about the future of their relationship. Judy had started to get very upset and, as usual, Tim had tried to calm her down. Predictably, Judy became even more upset. Finally, she had to go to work. When Judy arrived home late that night, they sat down to carry on the discussion, and again they seemed stuck. Tim told her that he had a surprise for her and asked her to close her eyes. He went into the kitchen, got a banana cream pie, and threw it in Judy's face! She was so shocked, she didn't know what to think. They had a good laugh over it when they told Pat. Although initially Judy wasn't thrilled to have banana cream pie all over her face, later she was pleased that Tim had been brave enough to take such a risk. Plus, she was impressed with his creativity. While this one action didn't solve their problems, it gave her the sense that maybe he could change, that he wasn't genetically a wimp. Ultimately, Tim was able to stand "toe-to-toe" with Judy during an argument, staying in the room with her even when his impulse was to flee.

The patterns that we do between people—relationship patterns—can be thought of as dances. If as a couple you are doing the tango and suddenly one of you decides to do the waltz, it is going to be very difficult for your partner to continue doing the tango. The good news about this is that *either partner can change the pattern*. If one partner changes her part of the pattern, the change creates a different context that is likely to change, or at least mess up, the old pattern. So, even if you can't get the one you love to read this book, you may be able to change your relationship by noticing and changing your part of the pattern.

Think about your relationship. What behaviors and interactions happen over and over again? Those are the patterns. Relationship patterns—be they good or bad—happen pretty much the same way again and again. If you have patterns that enhance your relationship, those are "solution patterns." A dual career couple we know leaves notes for each other. Besides the usual business of family life, the partners include messages about missing or loving the other. This pattern helps keep them connected even though they are busy; it is a solution pattern that strengthens their relationship.

And then there are patterns that don't work—"problem patterns." These are recurring interactions that one or both of you don't like or that hurt your relationship.

Problem Patterns

Many couples typically get into arguments over certain topics, like which baseball team is better, or how often the in-laws should visit. James Thurber once wrote a short story about a couple, the Winships, who got divorced because they had a conflict about whether Greta Garbo or Donald Duck was a better actor. We have seen couples separate or divorce over not much more than this. What topic usually gets one or both of you going? Our guess is that it is not just the topic but the way the discussion happens that generates heat (but no light). Are there typical tones of voice used in the discussion? Does the disagreement usually occur at a certain time, like late at night or just before a visit with the in-laws?

We'll take a look at these and other aspects of unworkable patterns. Because you probably won't be able to avoid the sensitive topics altogether (or that may be what you are arguing about—one partner wants to talk about it and the other doesn't), we focus on changing the aspects of the pattern that you have some control over—the things you *can* change. We begin by examining the anatomy of problem patterns, identifying those major elements that we have noticed over the years in our own and other couples' relationships. We focus on those parts of the patterns that you could see on a videotape. As always, we emphasize actions because those are more easily identified and changed than inner patterns of thinking and feeling.

Trigger Words or Phrases

There may be a phrase that triggers an argument. In the movie *Babe,* Babe Ruth's wife could get him to go ballistic by calling him "incorrigible." That term had been applied to him when he was young and had hurt him very deeply.

At the beginning of the book we pointed out that the labels derived from the self-help field can be particularly unhelpful when applied to someone else. It is one thing to say, "I am codependent," and quite another to say, "You are codependent," or "a man who hates women." You can imagine the argument patterns that are triggered by those phrases.

In one of our relationship classes, a couple talked about a trigger for their fights. As the couple dressed to go out for the evening a crisis would ensue when the wife asked, "Are you going to wear *that?*" Her husband got disgusted about her repetitious, indirect challenging of his wardrobe choices. One day as they were preparing to attend a wedding, she asked her usually provocative question. Without a word, he went back into the bedroom and emerged wearing colorful boxer shorts over his dress pants! It took a lot of begging and pleading on her part to get him to change before they went, as he fully intended to go dressed like that to teach her a lesson.

The problem pattern does not have to involve an argument. Phrases can trigger withdrawal or discouragement without a fight at all. One of Pat's friends said that he discovered after his divorce that as soon as someone tells him that she wants more closeness from him, he shuts down and withdraws from her.

Voice Tones and Volumes

Are your voice tones and voice volumes speaking volumes? Have you heard someone say to you, "It's not what you say, it's how you say it." As simple a phrase as "Nice outfit," with the right sarcastic inflection, could demoralize someone's self-concept for an entire evening. Voice volumes have to do with how loudly something is said. "I'm ready to go!" said loudly might be very intimidating, but spoken in a moderate voice volume it would simply be sharing useful information. Voice tones and volumes can interact. Loud volume and sarcastic tone—such as Steve Martin's "Well, *excuse* me!"—can be funny; said softly in your ear at a party, the same words have a completely different meaning.

It sometimes seems that we save the worst tones of voice for the ones we love. We speak to our partners or children in tones and volumes that we would never use with a stranger on the street. Bill had an experience that well illustrates this point.

I had just finished a session of marriage counseling with a couple who had been fighting constantly and were on the verge of a divorce. The session had been a good one. They had finally gotten through all the bitterness and realized how much they truly loved one another. They both cried as they reconnected with their love and I, too, was moved to tears. Their voice tones and volumes were such a contrast to the ones they had used with each other at the beginning of the session.

Then I stopped at the supermarket on the way home. I was just coming around the corner when I overheard a couple in the next aisle. The man was putting something into the grocery cart and the woman was saying harshly, "I told you we already had that!" They both looked a bit embarrassed when they realized that I had heard them. They reminded me of that couple I had just left. I guessed they probably loved one another, like the couple in my office, but the message of love certainly hadn't gotten through in that voice tone!

What channel are *you* broadcasting on? Do the voice tones and volumes you use get through to your partner the way you'd like?

Nonverbal Behaviors

Perhaps a nonverbal action (gesture, movement, posture, eye contact, etc.) of which you are unaware is part of your problem pattern.

Pat videotaped a marital therapy session with a couple who argued quite a bit during the consultation. In reviewing the tape she noticed that they never looked at each other when they were fighting, but made eye contact when they were getting along. During the next session, Pat showed them sections of the tape with the sound off and pointed out the pattern. She suggested that they look at each other when they started to get into a fight. They found that, whenever they made direct eye contact, the bitter arguing stopped.

One morning, just after we'd both awakened, Pat and I had a discussion that was starting to get heated. I kept pounding my finger on the bed to emphasize my point. Pat was getting more and more upset; then finally she realized what was happening. She asked me to stop pounding my finger, because she was starting to fear that I was getting too upset. I didn't agree that I was getting too upset or that, even if I did get upset, that would be such a bad thing. Pat told me that she was so distracted by the finger pounding that she couldn't really listen to the point I was making, so I agreed to stop pounding. It was hard, though. That finger seemed to have a mind of its own. After a few minutes, it started pounding again. I finally had to resort to sitting on my hand to finish the discussion.

Places

Sometimes the problem patterns occur only in a certain location, such as the car, the bedroom, or the kitchen.

Pat was working with Chuck and Marita. They complained of unproductive fights. Pat asked when and where they usually fought. The couple agreed that the verbal boxing ring was usually the kitchen. When Pat asked what typically started the fights, Chuck said, "She gives me her 'get-out-of-my-kitchen' look." Marita said, "I honestly don't know what look he is talking about." Pat suggested that, between now and the next session, Chuck could tell Marita every time she gave him the "get-out-of-my-kitchen look." He had three opportunities to point out the look. When he questioned Marita about the look, he discovered that only one of those three times was she actually thinking, "get out of my kitchen." Instead, she was thinking, "Why are those kids listening to that silly TV show in the next room?" or "Oh, no! I'm halfway through making this dish and I can't finish it without paprika, which I don't have." One of the three times, Chuck was accurate in guessing that Marita was thinking, "Get out of my kitchen." Even then, they didn't get into the old pattern of fighting, because instead of getting irritated, he asked Marita what she was thinking rather than assuming he knew and reacting. She told Chuck that she just wanted some time alone. He understood and was glad she had told him rather than just resenting his presence and expressing it nonverbally.

Times

Ted and LeeAnn had a pattern they enacted every evening during the work week. Ted would come home from work, wanting to spend some time just staring at the TV or reading the paper to relax. LeeAnn was home alone most of the day; also, since they had recently moved to the area, she had not yet developed friendships. She wanted to talk about their respective days the minute Ted arrived home. They ended up arguing almost every evening about whose needs were going to be met. He had begun to think that she was too needy and perhaps he had made a mistake in getting married. LeeAnn was starting to doubt herself and feel as if she were going crazy. She was also beginning to conclude, as she had read in a self-help book, that Ted was afraid of intimacy.

This couple hadn't noticed their pattern, that the arguments always occurred right after he arrived home from work. Because they were focused on their feelings, needs, or ideas about why things weren't working, they missed a simple truth hidden in the pattern and therefore a simple way to change it. We'll tell you how we helped them change this repeating pattern later in this chapter. Stay tuned.

Any Other Regularity

Do you feel like your relationship is in a rut? Perhaps one or both of you is bored. Do you repeat the same interactions again and again, so that you have stopped seeing each other for who you are? Do you only see your image of your partner? The difference between a rut and a grave is just the dimensions. Some relationships look as if they are pretty close to the grave when we see them. Hopefully yours is just in a rut and not ready for a grave. Changing your problem patterns can cause your rut to become a runway to new directions. We came across a quote (it was not attributed to an author, so if you know who wrote it, please let us know) while we were writing this chapter: "It is important not to mistake the edge of the rut for the horizon."

Identify one problem pattern that repeats again and again and start experimenting. Do something *unexpected*. Try changing your individual and relationship patterns to expand your horizons. We'll give you specific guidelines about things to do that break up and change your patterns in the next sections.

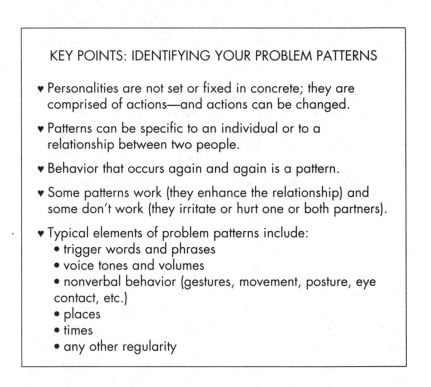

KEY POINTS: IDENTIFYING YOUR PROBLEM PATTERNS

♥ Personalities are not set or fixed in concrete; they are comprised of actions—and actions can be changed.

♥ Patterns can be specific to an individual or to a relationship between two people.

♥ Behavior that occurs again and again is a pattern.

♥ Some patterns work (they enhance the relationship) and some don't work (they irritate or hurt one or both partners).

♥ Typical elements of problem patterns include:
  • trigger words and phrases
  • voice tones and volumes
  • nonverbal behavior (gestures, movement, posture, eye contact, etc.)
  • places
  • times
  • any other regularity

> ## ACTION STEPS: NOTICING PROBLEM PATTERNS
>
> ⇨ For the next week, notice what you do when your partner is upset that leads to results or responses you don't like.
>
> ⇨ Make a list of words, phrases, voice tones or volumes, gestures, postures, etc., that trigger a negative response from your partner.
>
> ⇨ Where do your problems usually occur? If it's at home, in what part of the house?
>
> ⇨ Notice the typical times of the day or days of the week that you have problems.

Changing Patterns

The first rule of holes:
When you are in one, stop digging.
Molly Ivins

There are several ways to change patterns in your relationship. You can use humor, you can change your nonverbal behaviors (body movements, eye contact, or voice tones), or you can change the location or timing of a pattern. The main thing to remember is, *if you do what you have always done, you're likely to get what you've always gotten.*

The starting point for changing a pattern is to ask yourself, "What do I usually do when my partner does what he or she does?" And then stop doing that; do something new. When what you are doing is not getting you the results you want, don't blame the other person or yourself—do something different. Start to experiment until you find something that changes the pattern. This is one exciting part of the *Stop Blaming, Start Loving* approach: one person can change the relationship, even if the other stays the same or seems unwilling to work on the relationship. Remember, it's hard to do the tango when your partner is doing the fox trot or the twist. This section is about learning some new dance steps.

Use Humor

Humor is one of our favorite ways of breaking patterns. I had the annoying habit of picking lint off Pat's clothes. After mentioning this to me in passing a couple of times with no results, Pat came up with a plan. Selecting a purple sweater that had pockets in it, unbeknownst to me, she put a spool of light blue thread in the pocket and then, using a sewing needle, ran thread underneath the body of the sweater and through a random spot on the sleeve. Later, as we were driving down the road with our kids (who had been tipped off to the joke) sitting in the back seat, I absentmindedly started to pick the thread off Pat's sweater. Greatly puzzled, I found myself pulling and pulling—until the laughter from behind me made it absolutely clear that I had been *had!* I now think twice before picking any lint off Pat's clothing.

One time Pat's father, Lofton, came into the kitchen and patted his wife Jessie on the bottom. She continued doing the dishes, apparently taking no notice. Lofton then walked over and patted the refrigerator. Jessie turned around, puzzle, and asked, "What are you doing?" Lofton replied, "I'm just trying to see if I can get more response from the refrigerator than I got from you." She laughed and gave him a hug.

Change Your Nonverbal Behaviors

Study your nonverbal behaviors and discover what voice tones or volumes, gestures, posture, and patterns of eye contact typically get a negative response from your partner. At what point does your partner explode, withdraw, or get defensive? Try changing *anything* about your nonverbal behavior. We are not giving you rules for what to do or not to do nonverbally (like, "Never cross your arms during a discussion because it indicates you are closed to the other person's point of view"). You and your partner (not us or any other professional) are the experts on what nonverbal behavior means to each of you. Only by observing and experimenting can you find what works (or doesn't) for your particular relationship.

One time in the middle of a disagreement, Pat reached over and touched me lightly on the leg. Instantly I became more relaxed and less defensive. I realized later that her touch had been reassuring to me, as if she were saying, "We're disagreeing now, but I still love you and I'm going to stay in the relationship with you."

Sometimes simply naming the nonverbal behavior changes it. As the mother of four children, I heard them discuss how much they disliked the "witch eyes" look that I got when I was angry. Their teasing me about the look made it impossible for me to use it— particularly after they had me practice it in a mirror!

David and Jan wanted to stop bickering. Pat suggested that when they found themselves contradicting each other, they simply hold hands. David and Jan found that they just couldn't keep the argument going if they were touching each other. Other couples have said that when they are angry they can't stand to touch each other, but it worked for David and Jan.

Sara had been in a dangerously abusive marriage before her present marriage to Rick. Whenever Rick looked angry, Sara would become immobilized with fear and have flashbacks of her frightening history. Pat worked with both of them. She encouraged Rick to practice various faces in the mirror so he could learn to control what look was on his face. Sara was to watch Rick practicing and tell him which facial expressions scared her. Seeing those faces in a non-conflict context helped Sara to change her reaction to angry looks and helped Rick learn which expressions got a better reaction from Sara.

One therapist we know bought foam rubber clown noses for a couple to wear when they started to bicker. The nonverbal humorous message of the clown noses changed the context from irritation to playfulness. Eventually they would say to each other, "Is it bozo time?" and it would stop an argument.

Change Your Location

Couples can alter the patterns of their problems by changing the location in which the pattern typically occurs. If you live in a cold climate, agree to go into an unheated garage if you start to have a fight. If one of the problems is that your children are overhearing the fights, you might go out to the car when you start to fight.

At a seminar, a man came up to Bill during a break and said he'd been to one of Bill's previous seminars. He had been doing marriage counseling with a couple, Ron and Penny, who had been having terrible fights in which they would both say hurtful things that they later regretted but which were hard to forgive. After trying everything he could think of to help this couple, the therapist finally stopped trying to determine the cause of the problem and decided to try to change their pattern. He suggested that the next time Ron and Penny started to say mean things to one another, they should immediately stop the argument and go into the bathroom. There Ron should take off all his clothes and lie down in the bathtub. Penny should sit above him on the toilet with all her clothes on, and they then should continue the argument. Well, as you might imagine, it was very difficult to continue the fight in that crazy situation. They would usually end up laughing at the absurdity of it all. After a while, a glance towards the bathroom was sufficient to defuse an argument.

Of course, we usually don't recommend going to such absurd lengths to change relationship patterns, but it worked for Ron and Penny.

Change Your Timing

Another possibility is to change the timing of the problem pattern. Can you find another time to bring up a sensitive subject other than right before your partner leaves for work? Do you typically wait to have sex until late at night when both of you are exhausted?

Remember the couple, Ted and LeeAnn, we mentioned earlier in the chapter, who had fights every weeknight? Ted wanted time to be alone and "space out," and LeeAnn wanted contact and conversation the minute he walked in the door. After we helped them discover the pattern, LeeAnn decided that she would plan to take a shower right after Ted arrived home. This would help her calm down and give her something to do, while at the same time it gave Ted enough time to relax. Then Ted decided that he would be extra attentive for the first fifteen minutes after LeeAnn emerged from the shower, so that she wouldn't feel neglected or ignored. By changing the timing of their actions, they were able to eliminate their problem pattern.

Bert and Susan found themselves feeling very discouraged about how their sex life had changed since the birth of their baby. Bert was a night owl and Susan was typically up at the crack of dawn. The timing was not supportive of their sex life, but before the baby they had been able to accommodate their differences. Now that there was a tiny observer who sapped their energy, the time for sex had become nearly impossible. Susan

*would want sex in the morning, when Bert was too tired to have
an erection, and she didn't like the idea that she should forego
even twenty minutes of sleep to make love. Finally they started
meeting at their apartment for "lunch" twice a week to keep
their sex life alive.*

Change Any Regularity

What happens over and over again in predictable ways in your
relationship? If you can discover regularities in your action patterns,
you can try changing one aspect and find out whether that one
aspect changes the problem. Often, it will. One place to search for
such regularities is in your partner's typical complaints about you.
Bill received enlightenment one day while doing marriage counseling with Catherine and James.

Catherine was complaining that James never fixed things around
the house. He agreed that he didn't fix things, but maintained that
he never noticed that things were broken until Catherine called his
attention to them. But she was reluctant to call his attention to
needed repairs, she said, because it felt like the burden was still on
her to initiate the repairs. As I was helping them, I realized that Pat
regularly complained about the same thing. When I got home, I
was determined to break this pattern by asking Pat to take me
around the house and tell me where she thought it needed work.
Pat wondered if someone had substituted a look-alike for her husband, because the Bill she knew would never do such a thing. With
my list in hand, I proceeded to fix things around the house and call
repair people to do several jobs that were beyond my expertise.

We often think of a relationship as a bank account. When you do
things your spouse loves, you are making a deposit; when you mess
up, you are making a withdrawal. Bill made a deposit in the relationship bank that lasted for months. (No overdrafts for him!) He
also didn't have to hear the old record, "You never fix anything
around here. The burden for taking care of the house is all on my

shoulders." (At least for a couple of months, until he had cashed a few more checks.)

One couple we knew was having serious difficulties. During an argument, the wife, Jean, would say terrible, cruel things to her husband, Curt. She would threaten to castrate him, saying that he wasn't a man. Pat was curious about how Curt responded to this verbal abuse. He would typically stand silently and take the berating. He said he felt completely deflated when she talked to him like that. Pat suggested that he could get creative and change his part of the pattern.

Curt had mentioned that these fights usually occurred in the kitchen. "Well, one thing you could do is crawl under the kitchen table and hide," Pat suggested. He hadn't thought of that, he admitted, but would be interested to see what effect it would have. Pat said, "Or you could get a water pistol and squirt Jean." He said, "Yeah, I never thought of that either—I could do that."

Curt tried hiding under the table; he tried squirting his wife with a water pistol. Both of those experiments worked—Jean laughed at them and stopped berating him. She had a great sense of humor. Pat also suggested that Curt leave the house for an hour when Jean started saying abusive things to him. This change also interrupted their pattern.

Pat asked Curt, "Have you ever thought of saying to Jean, 'Boy, that really hurts my feelings when you say that'?" He said, "No, I don't say anything." So she said, "Well, you might try that."

The next time this pattern erupted, Curt found a way to tell Jean how he felt. Somehow, in the more than twenty years they had been together, Jean had never considered how painful it was for Curt when she spoke to him with such cruelty. She was deeply moved by his disclosure. A productive discussion followed, breaking their pattern of withdrawing from one another after one of these incidents.

When you notice patterns in your relationship, you can not only discover what is *not* working but also recall what worked in the past, or in other situations, and implement those helpful patterns again. Next we will show you how to use these helpful patterns to renew and recharge your relationship.

KEY POINTS: CHANGING PROBLEM PATTERNS

♥ Problem patterns can be changed by picking one behavior you do repeatedly and altering it.

♥ You can change your problem patterns by using humor, changing your nonverbal behaviors (voice tone and volume, gestures, posture, eye contact, etc.), or changing location or timing in the problem situation.

♥ One person can change a two-person pattern.

♥ When what you are doing is not producing the result you want, don't blame your partner or yourself—*do something different.* Experiment until you find a behavior that works.

ACTION STEPS: CHANGING PROBLEM PATTERNS

⇨ Use humor as an unexpected element.

⇨ Change the location in which you typically enact your problem pattern. Go to the bathroom or the garage instead of having your usual fight in the kitchen.

⇨ Change the voice tones and volumes, gestures, or postures you have been using in the problem patterns.

Solution Patterns

We have been emphasizing changing patterns that don't work. Sometimes, however, it is even more helpful to find patterns that *do* work. These are your solution patterns. You may have used them once and forgotten about them or you may use them in one setting, like with friends or at work, but not in your relationship. You can find solution patterns in lots of places, present or past.

Solution Patterns from Your Work Place

Diane had taken her car to the mechanic to have the clutch replaced for the second time. The service manager at the auto shop decided to make sure that this was the last clutch he ever had to replace for Diane. He showed her how to adjust the clutch, he joked with her about having her tools with her at all times (her fingers), and he took her for a short ride to demonstrate exactly how to drive in a way that would preserve her clutch. After Diane arrived home that evening, she asked Ted, her husband, for help with something on their home computer. "I showed you how to do this last week!" he barked at her. The difference was striking to her and she was hurt that her own husband had treated her worse than the service manager. Ted, who had a small business and knew about customer service, didn't transfer his work skills to his personal life. He possessed a solution he was using at work but not at home.

Do you lose your temper at work the way you do at home? Probably not. Do you have effective ways to manage conflicts at work that you seem to forget when you are in your romantic relationship? Probably. One place to search for solution patterns is at work. Pay attention to what you do in your job that produces good results. Observe yourself—how do you handle challenges and conflicts? Try using some of those action patterns at home with your partner.

Bill and I used to have an annual fight when it came time to get ready for the Christmas party. I wanted everything to be as perfect as possible: the house was to be decorated perfectly, cleaned perfectly, and food prepared perfectly. Bill, who is not as exacting as I am in these matters, usually resented being asked to participate in the preparation, because he felt that he would spend his whole day trying in vain to meet my Christmas standards. After fighting about this for the first three years we were married, we found another pattern that worked. I remembered that when I wanted his input on a writing project, if I asked him, "Would you help?" I usually got a "no." But if I asked, "Would you proof these two pages?" I got a "yes." So, rather than lecturing Bill or making a vague general request, I asked, "Are you willing to devote three hours on the day of the Christmas party to getting ready?" Bill was very agreeable to this. This solution to the annual Christmas party fight worked so well that now, twenty or thirty parties of various sorts later, we use this pattern every time.

Bob and Susan came for marital therapy in crisis, on the verge of divorce. Susan had threatened to leave and Bob was desperate to convince her to stay. Since Bob was an entrepreneur, Bill asked him what he would do if his business were in trouble and his customers were threatening to defect to another company if they did not see some major improvements in quality and service. Bob described in detail the time and the attention he would put into his job and give his customers in order to keep his business thriving. Bill suggested that Bob's marriage was now in Chapter 11 (bankruptcy lite) and asked him to work to save his marriage using ideas and tactics based on his business expertise. It was as if a bright light had switched on for Bob. Before he had been mystified and resentful of his wife's complaints; now he saw what he could do and was energized and ready to work.

Solution Patterns from Friendships

Solutions patterns often abound in a context of nonsexual relationships. Noticing what succeeds with friends can help you find action patterns that will improve your marital relationship.

> *Jan was upset when her husband was twenty minutes late for dinner at a restaurant where they had agreed to meet. She attacked him for being late and pointed out that his mother was always late too. Later she thought, "If my friend Mary had been twenty minutes late, I at least would have let her explain and I certainly would not have jumped on her about her parents."*

When you are in conflict with your spouse, ask yourself, "How would I behave with a friend in a situation like this?" By studying and using your friendship model for solution patterns, you will discover that you already have skills you can draw upon to change patterns in your romantic relationship.

> *Matt and Jenny were newlyweds who fought over how often they would spend time with their respective parents. They attended the relationship class we teach, where we talked about discovering what happens when you look for solutions from other areas of your life. As they discussed their problem pattern, they realized that the same simple courtesy they would extend to their friends would be a way to avoid fighting. If either of them invited the other to go to their parents, instead of announcing, "We are going to Mom's for dinner," the other was much more likely to agree to the in-law time.*

Solution Patterns from Your History Together

Search in your relationship for times when you felt closer. What was going on then? What were you or your spouse doing that you have stopped doing or are doing less these days? Look back at the very beginning of your relationship to remind you what worked better. When you were first in love, you probably took more time for romance, for sex, and for talk about your relationship. One woman we know said that when she was first with her husband, he made her a huge heart for Valentine's Day and then pasted pasta letters (the dry ones used to make alphabet soup) onto a cardboard heart to tell her how much he loved her.

While such heroic efforts may not be appropriate for your current lifestyle, maybe you could try going out to dinner like you used to, lying in bed a while on a Sunday afternoon, or taking the time to comment on how nice your partner looks.

KEY POINTS: FINDING SOLUTION PATTERNS

♥ Search in other contexts for patterns that are helpful to your relationship.

♥ Patterns that are successful in your job can be applied to your relationship.

♥ Patterns from friendships can provide a model for your marriage.

♥ Consider reinstating patterns that worked earlier in your relationship.

ACTION STEPS: NOTICING SOLUTION PATTERNS

⇨ For the next week, write down things that happened at work or in your friendships that added enjoyment or eased conflicts. Use any of these patterns to improve your relationship.

⇨ For the next week, notice the things your partner does when you are upset that resolve or soften conflict.

⇨ With your partner, discuss things that you two did early in your relationship that increased your feelings of love or resolved conflict.

How to Be Smarter Than a Rat

There is a story that captures the essence of what we've suggested in this chapter. A man went in search of wisdom in this life. He wanted to find out about people and the world and how everything worked. He explored many different disciplines. He studied physical disciplines such as yoga, athletics, and martial arts. He sought enlightenment in spiritual disciplines, going from one religion to another. He investigated academic disciplines like mathematics, physics, chemistry, medicine, economics, geography, philosophy, and geology. After searching long and diligently, he finally came to psychology. By then he had figured out that there was a lot of speculation and a lot of stories about how the world worked. He really wanted to discover what psychology had to offer so that he could quickly move on to the next area of pursuit. He went to the library and he looked for a book that he thought would cut to the heart of the matter. He found a book on the bookshelf that he thought would do just that. It was called *Things Psychology Has*

Proven (it was a fairly slim volume). Well, anyway, he opened it, started reading it, and learned that mainly psychology has proven only that you can teach rats to run mazes.

Most undergraduate psychology students have conducted these experiments, which are done in the rat lab. The experimenter takes a rat and puts it at the beginning of the maze, which is a labyrinth with four possible exits. (You have to starve the rat to motivate it to search the maze for food.) There are different slots at the end of the four exits so you can create different experiments by placing the reward (cheese or pellets) at different exits. All the slots are closed at the start of the experiment. To start an experiment, you choose an exit. For example, you pick up slot number four and put some cheese down at the end of that slot.

Down the first tunnel the little rat scurries and finds no exit and no food. The rat's hungry, so it goes back to the second tunnel. No exit, no cheese. Third tunnel; no exit, no cheese. Down at the end of the fourth tunnel it finds the exit and the cheese. Return the rat to its cage, starve it some more, return it to the beginning of the maze. Put the food at the end of the fourth tunnel again. First tunnel, no cheese, second tunnel, third tunnel, no cheese. Finally, it gets to the fourth tunnel and gets the cheese. After a couple of times, you get a smart rat. Now when you put the rat at the beginning of the maze, it runs right down the fourth tunnel. No question about it—the rat doesn't bother with any other tunnel on the first try. The student records how many trials it takes for the rat to learn this. Then the psychology student closes slot number four and records how long it takes to extinguish this behavior—how long it takes the rat to unlearn going down the fourth tunnel and to learn a new pattern.

This time the student picks up slot number two and puts the cheese down there. The rat is placed at the beginning of the maze. By now the rat has learned the cheese is *always* down the fourth tunnel, so it runs right down the fourth tunnel. This time, no exit and no food. The rat returns to the beginning, thinking (we guess) that it must have made a mistake. The rat goes back down the fourth tunnel again but, again, no exit and no cheese. Back and forth, back and forth goes the rat as the student records its efforts. Eventually the rat gives up going down the fourth tunnel and tries the first tunnel again, and tries the second tunnel and finds the cheese. Soon the rat automatically goes down the second tunnel.

The man in search of wisdom closed the book on psychology, put it back on the shelf, and thought, "There is only a limited amount that I can take from this book in my quest for wisdom about people and how the world works, because I already know that there's a *big* difference between rats and human beings. Rats, if they get hungry, will eventually go down a different tunnel, but human beings will go down the fourth tunnel again, and again, and again, thinking that the cheese will be there eventually." Sometimes they even pull up a chair at the end of the fourth tunnel and just sit there and think, "I'll just hang out here—I'm sure the cheese will be here sooner or later. It was here in the family that I grew up in, it was here in my last relationship, so I'm sure it will be here this time." Or, "My stories tell me that the cheese will show up here or that it should be here, so I'll just wait here." Rats—they don't know from anything but cheese. All they want to know about in the end is getting the results—cheese. But human beings could eat their stories for decades, never getting the outcomes they want, as far as we can tell. Oftentimes we're not getting what we want, yet we keep doing the same old pattern, thinking, "If only I do it harder or louder, my partner will finally realize and correct the error of his (or her) ways."

When things go wrong in our relationships, we are all inclined to look at our mates and conclude that *they* have got the personality problem, and if only they would fix the problem, everything would be better. If it's not a personality problem, perhaps it's a life event. "He's never worked through his father's death and he takes it out on me." Or, "She has a conflict with her boss, but I get the flack." The difficulty with this line of thinking is that we will continue to see our mates as the cause of the pattern and nothing will change. It's difficult to escape from the problem when viewed in this manner, because you can't change history and it's hard to change your partner's personality. We are suggesting, however, that there is an escape route from a pattern that doesn't work. The escape route is to figure out what you keep doing over and over again (individually and as a couple) and simply *do something different*. Rita Mae Brown wrote, "Insanity is doing the same thing over and over and expecting different results." You can get out of the pattern that you're stuck in by changing *what* you are doing—not by changing who you are or who your partner is, but by changing *what you do* individually in the relationship and/or what you both do when you are having problems. Maybe someday we humans can become smarter than rats.

INTEGRITY, LIMITS, AND CONSEQUENCES

What to Do When Relationship Patterns Are Destructive

Some patterns are more than annoying or frustrating—they are potentially or actually destructive. So far in this book, we've assumed that both of you are motivated and willing to make efforts to improve your relationship. Here we deal with situations in which you (or your partner) engages in behavior that threatens or destroys the relationship (affairs, physical violence, drug and alcohol problems, compulsive gambling, etc.). We provide non-blaming, hopeful ways to change such dangerous patterns. We also help you decide when it is unrealistic to expect change to happen and how to sever the relationship.

This chapter is divided into two sections. The first part focuses on what to do if *you* have violated the trust in your relationship. The second section tells you what to do if *your partner* betrays your trust or becomes violent. We suggest actions to take to restore the safety and trust in the relationship or to realize that it is time to get out of it.

The word *integrity* comes from the same root as the word *integration*. Without integrity you feel divided within yourself. In order to feel one with yourself, not split, you need to act in a way that is in accord with your values.

Integrity has three levels. The first involves keeping your word and staying within the agreed-upon limits. The second level requires accountability for breaking your word or violating the personal boundaries of another. On the third level you make amends when you have hurt your partner or damaged the trust and safety in the relationship.

Keeping Your Word and Respecting Limits and Boundaries

Maintaining your integrity is simple: *do what you say you will do and don't do what you say you won't do.* If you say that you are not going to have sex with anyone other than your partner, then do not have sex with anyone else. If you say that you are going to put your paycheck in the bank, put your paycheck in the bank. If you say you are not going to gamble, don't. Keep your word and respect the limits you have agreed to abide by. (Of course, there are also limits to which most adults do not explicitly agree but which are assumed, such as the implicit understanding that it is not acceptable for an adult to have sex with a child.) Most of the problems couples have in this area involve violations of explicit agreements. In a relationship in which there has been a problem with integrity, the first step is to clarify the boundaries and the agreements.

Debbie and Jim had been married for five years. They had married right out of college and Jim had gone into his family's lucrative business. In the first three years of their marriage, they had continued to engage in the same kind of party life they had

*enjoyed in college. Jim liked to gamble and drink, and as long as
this behavior did not prevent Debbie from pursuing her graduate
work, she did not object. Then their son Jason was born. Suddenly everything shifted for Debbie. Now she no longer wanted
to be a party girl, she was a mom; now Jim's drinking and gambling, which used to be so fun, seemed immature and irresponsible. Jim resented her changing the rules. He particularly resented
her wanting him to stop gambling. That felt like control to him.
The final straw for Debbie had been Jim's missing a house pay-
ment because he had gambled. Debbie became disgusted and
wanted Jim to go to a Gamblers Anonymous group. Jim resisted
and she, having read up on gambling addiction, accused him of
being "in denial." They were stuck. With our help, they agreed
on new limits. Jim would have a separate bank account for his
gambling. He could put $400 a month along with any earnings
he got from his gambling into that account, but he would not
touch any other money for gambling. If he did dip into the family coffers for his gambling, then he agreed he would go to the
gambling addiction group. Jim surprised all of us by keeping the
agreement. There were still other things that needed to be
worked on in the relationship, such as more equal parenting,
communication, and sex, but with that limit-setting the integrity
issue was resolved.*

If Debbie had said, "I want you to be more mature," or insisted
that he admit that he was "addicted to gambling," she would have
gotten nowhere with Jim. Lectures and labels had been tried on
Jim, with no success. When Debbie made the boundaries clear and
Jim agreed to the limits, he had an opportunity to show that he
could keep his word.

It is important, then, to make the agreement clear so that both
parties know when one or the other is keeping his or her word and
when not. By using videotalk to describe what constitutes "infidelity," what indicates "drinking too much," what is "being irresponsible about money," you and your partner can clearly define

the limits and boundaries of integrity for each other. Does it constitute "infidelity" to kiss another person or is penis-vagina contact
required for infidelity? Is it okay to tell another person intimate
details about your partner? Is "drinking too much" having four
beers at a party or is anything over a six-pack per day too much? Is
it "irresponsible" to buy your spouse an expensive present and put
it on the credit card to pay it off over time? If you want to be certain
that there are no misunderstandings and that both of you know the
boundaries, translate ambiguities into videotalk.

Accountability in Relationships

We distinguish blame from accountability in our work with couples. Blame means that you label the person or the person's intentions negatively; accountability means that people are responsible
for their previous actions and accountable for making amends and
changing their actions in the future. Integrity happens when an
individual acknowledges his or her accountability and stops doing
actions that lack integrity.

Pat and I came from similar backgrounds, but as a young adult I
was somewhat poor. Now that I've become more financially secure, I sometimes indulge myself. (When we were writing this, Pat
wondered if *sometimes* was the right word.) Pat considers spending
money on anything you can't eat, live in, or wear to be extravagant
behavior.

In the mail I received a solicitation from American Express for a
platinum card. I had heard of a gold card but never a platinum
card—that's the step above, or so the ad implied. I thought, *It's
$250 a year, but what the heck—I'd like one of these things. I'd enjoy the
status.* All I had to do was sign my name to apply, so I sent in the
application, assuming that I would be turned down. Although I had
always paid my credit card bills, more often than not I'd paid them
late.

About a week later Pat and I were sitting in bed and Pat was going through her mail. She had gotten the same solicitation under her name, and as she opened it, I heard her say, "What *idiot* would pay $250 for a ridiculous status symbol like this platinum American Express card!" She tossed it in the wastebasket with disgust.

I was thinking, *Well, I know one.* But banking on the likelihood that I would never get approved anyway, I decided not to bring it up. Pat would just be upset with me for my indulgence and, since I was probably not going to be approved anyway, why cause unnecessary conflict.

Soon after that, I went away to Europe on an extended teaching trip. When I returned, my mail had accumulated. Going through it, I found a notice saying, "Did you receive your platinum card? If not, call this number." *So I got approved, surprise!* I went through the rest of my mail. No platinum card. I called American Express and said, "I got this letter asking whether I had received my card, but I haven't received it. I was overseas for a couple of weeks, so maybe it got misplaced." They asked me if anyone else had handled my mail while I was gone and I said, "Only my family." They said, "Will you check with all your family members to see if they have set it aside for you?" After a pause, I asked, "Do I *have* to?" They said, "Yes, sir, you really do need to."

I checked first with all of the kids, but none of them had seen it. When Pat came home that night, I decided to make a clean breast of it. "I have something I need to talk to you about," I confessed. "Remember a couple of weeks ago when you said, 'What idiot would spend $250 for the platinum American Express card?' Well, *I'm* one of those idiots."

"Oh, Bill," Pat replied disapprovingly.

Immediately defensive, I countered, "Well, see, this is why I didn't tell you, because of your voice tone. I knew you'd disapprove and we'd just get into a hassle about it."

"Spending this $250 is a ridiculous indulgence and something you don't need," Pat answered. "I think you're wasting money.

Although I don't like that, it's not a big deal. What really scares me is that you would withhold information from me. Now I wonder what else you've withheld from me and whether I can trust you."

As to the mysterious disappearance of the card, Pat told me that she had thrown away an envelope from American Express, assuming it was a solicitation for one of those stupid platinum cards I surely wouldn't want.

This experience helped me learn to stand up for what I wanted. I realized I had undermined my own integrity, thinking Pat might disapprove. It would have been much better if I had said, "I want this platinum card even though I know you don't approve of it." Eventually it came to that anyway, because American Express sent a replacement. This time I stood up for what I wanted and Pat, after expressing her viewpoint, was not interested in whether or not I wasted the money, only that I tell her the truth and not withhold information. Keeping peace at the price of one's integrity makes the peace too high a price.

> *Pat was working with Carla, whose husband, Phil, was known for his frugality. (That's a polite way of saying that he was cheap.) This was a second marriage for Carla. When Phil had refused to help her with his stepson's college expenses, she had secretly taken out a loan for $10,000. Pat was concerned that Phil would one day be sitting at a desk at a mortgage company, arranging for refinancing, when up on a computer screen would pop this loan information. It was likely that withholding the information would damage the marriage more than the loan itself. Carla did tell Phil about the loan. He was upset, but after he recovered from the initial shock he was happy that she had told him.*

We are often asked if people should tell their partners when they have broken agreements. Be it spending more money than you had agreed upon, losing something your partner valued, getting drunk while out of town, or having an affair, for us the guideline is: if anything you have done and not discussed makes you feel separated from your partner, then telling him or her is probably best. We have worked with many spouses over the years who were more distraught about the cover-up by their mates than they were about the original transgression.

> *Nancy found out that Sam was having an affair with Rose. He quickly broke off the extramarital relationship and assured Nancy that it did not mean that much to him. Nancy felt upset about the betrayal, of course, but what really unnerved her was realizing the number of times Sam had deceived her by routinely lying about his whereabouts. Naively believing and trusting him, she now felt like such a sucker.*

When you acknowledge that you have broken your word or exceeded the agreed-upon limits, do so without blaming your partner or making excuses. Be accountable for what *you* have done.

> *Jay and Megan had separated due to Jay's violent behavior. When they were discussing the incident, Jay had said defensively, "Sure, I slapped you. I think it was a reaction." His wording implied that somehow she had made him hit her.*

That is not accountability—that's *blame*. Accountability means acknowledging what *you* did.

> *When Julie and Will had been married ten years, Will had an affair that nearly destroyed the marriage, not just because of the betrayal, but because Will refused to admit, "Yes, I did it and I was wrong." He kept implying that the affair was Julie's fault. In spite of his blaming behavior, they were eventually able to put the affair behind them and continue with their married life. The*

day of their 25th wedding anniversary, Will, out of the blue, apologized to Julie for having had the affair and especially for having blamed Julie for it. "It was never your fault. I was foolish, please forgive me." Julie said that was the best anniversary present she could possibly have received.

Once you've acknowledged your breach of integrity and taken responsibility for it, the next step is to make amends and to take whatever actions are necessary to restore trust in the relationship.

Making Amends

One of the steps in recovery in Alcoholics Anonymous involves making amends for the hurt and injury you caused to others while drinking. We have found that this step is just as useful in marital therapy as in AA groups. If you have broken the trust in your relationship, find some kind of action to restore or at least mend the broken trust. If you have been violent, you might offer to join a group for abusers. If you've had an affair, you might let your partner open all your mail for the next year to ensure that the person with whom you had the affair is not contacting you. One man offered to let his wife call or visit him at any time while he was at work or any social event to reassure her that he was no longer lying to her. A woman wrote her partner an apology for having been violent and promised never to get physically abusive again in the relationship.

When Nancy found out about Sam's affair, she began to obsess about where Sam was every single minute. Was he with Rose? Was he talking to her on the phone? Rose lived in a nearby community, so the telephone call would be long distance. Sam decided to be hyperaccountable to Nancy for his whereabouts. He said, "I have nothing to hide, so you are wel-

come to open my mail, check my long distance bill, or call me anytime. I want you to learn to trust me again, and if being accountable for my time will help you, then I am glad to do it." Nancy still worried a bit and did occasionally check the phone bill and his clothing, but Sam's willingness to be accountable helped reassure her.

You may wonder if you will ever be able to regain the trust once it has been lost in your relationship. We've seen many marriages in which trust was restored, so our answer is yes. Pat's father used to say, "Trust is based on positive predictability over time." When the agreements between you are clear and ethical behavior is unambiguously defined, then trust *can* be reestablished. But don't expect instant results just because you have apologized. People who have affairs often think, "No one will be hurt by this," but when the affair is discovered, the betrayed spouse is often haunted by flashbacks, just like people who suffer from post-traumatic stress (such as war veterans and rape victims). Healing may take years. The actions we suggest in this chapter and the next are designed to facilitate this healing—but be patient.

KEY POINTS: THE THREE LEVELS OF INTEGRITY

♥ Keep your word and stay within agreed-upon limits.

♥ If you break your word or violate the limits, be accountable for your actions.

♥ Offer to make amends and find actions that reestablish trust and set secure limits.

ACTIONS STEPS: PRESERVING OR RESTORING INTEGRITY

⇨ Discuss the limits of acceptable behavior in some potential or actual problem area with your partner. Get a clear description (in videotalk) about the limits and what will constitute a violation of the agreement.

⇨ If you have broken your word or violated the trust in your relationship, acknowledge it to your partner and let him or her know that you take responsibility for your actions.

⇨ If you have broken your word or violated the trust in your relationship, offer to make amends. Be hyperaccountable if that's what it takes to restore the trust. Ask your partner what actions you could do to make things right or to reestablish trust. Don't expect the trust to be instantly restored. It will probably take some time of consistent, trustworthy behavior on your part to reassure your partner.

Out of Bounds

So far we have focused on what to do when *you* have blown it. What do you do when your partner is the one who has breached the integrity? What if you have a partner who is repeatedly or chronically engaged in destructive behaviors (such as affairs, physical violence, drug and alcohol abuse, compulsive gambling, and so on) or who refuses to change when there are serious problems in the relationship? Our guideline for dealing with these kinds of problems is to bypass blame and story-making, instead holding your partner accountable and giving him or her a chance to change. That can be a challenge when violence is involved, but let's give it a try.

An interesting point about violence came to our attention in an excellent book by Carol Tavris, *Anger: The Misunderstood Emotion*. She noted that in a national sample of 2,143 American families, 12 percent of women and 12 percent of men reported becoming violent when they were angry. Those statistics fit Pat's experience on a radio talk show in which she discussed the topic of domestic violence. In addition to the expected women callers, three men called in who had experienced violence at the hands of their wives (having a lamp thrown, having been hit with a baseball bat, and having been cut with a knife). Men are often reluctant to speak about the violence they experience from women, perhaps because they fear appearing weak and assume they wouldn't be believed. Men seem to have gotten a reputation as brutes because they more often use fists, guns, and knives whereas women punch, slap, and throw things. Male violence more often results in greater damage and death than female violence. Also, many women still have less income than men and are socialized to feel more responsible for childrearing, so they often stay in violent relationships longer than men. The fact that a similar percentage of women as men regularly behave violently in a home setting is why our guidelines for breaking the cycle of violence do not focus on one gender or the other.

One common problem in violent situations is that of blaming the victim. The person who is abused is blamed for the violence that is inflicted upon him or her. We believe that in a family or a relationship, no one is to blame and everyone is accountable. This means that each person in a relationship can do his or her part to stop violence and that the person who gets violent is responsible for his or her actions, regardless of what preceded those actions.

What we do we mean when we say that the victim of the violence is also accountable? Even if you are being abused, you have options. You can develop and use an escape plan; you can tell a friend, co-worker, or family member what is going on (there is some evidence that "going public"—breaking the silent, shameful secret of domestic violence—is one effective way to change it); you can get a job even though your partner might object, since having your own money may help increase your options for escape; you can call the police; and you can avoid striking the first blow. The point is, whether you are victim or victimizer, you have choices, however small, about your actions. Your accountability can be found within the range of those choices. Some people leave abusive situations; not everyone stays. If you have stayed this long, do not blame yourself. Just begin to take steps either to stop the abuse or get away from it.

Holding the violent partner accountable means not accepting any excuses that minimize responsibility in the situation or suggest no other choices were available. We have listened to a variety of explanations and rationalizations from partners who get violent:

"My father beat the hell out of us all when we were kids, so I guess I just learned that way to deal with anger. I can't help it. When I get mad, I strike out."

"She goaded me into it."

"Everybody hits their wife sometimes. It's no big deal."

"He's a big man and I'm just a little woman. So I throw things at him when I get mad. It evens the odds."

We are generally optimistic about the possibilities for changing harmful patterns in relationships, but we have found severe domestic violence to be the hardest marital problem to tackle. Particularly frightening are the cases in which the violence happens repeatedly and at times seems to come out of nowhere. Worse still, some partners show no remorse after violent episodes. The only course of action in such situations is to do your best to escape alive. If you are in an abusive relationship, we know it may be extremely difficult to get out. You may feel as if you will never get out alive, or that even if you get out, you still will not be safe. People who are not in your situation cannot fully relate to your fear, self-doubt, humiliation, and the sense of entrapment. Nevertheless, if you are reading these words, we can tell you that many people do make it out alive and, once they are out, find their way back to safety and self-respect.

In the more typical cases of spouses who get violent in the middle of an argument but regret it afterwards, we have had some success with the following plan of escalating consequences.

Reaffirm the Limits and Boundaries

Instead of giving your spouse a label when he or she is behaving destructively or unethically in your marriage, focus on identifying specific limits and then stick with those limits. Whether or not the label you chose for your mate is valid is not the issue. You may be right. He may be a "sex addict" or a "sociopath." She may have a "Cinderella Complex" or "love too much." The problem is that labels generally imply blame, invalidation, or reduce the possibilities for change, and they don't tell you how to change things if your partner doesn't accept the label. Often the fight becomes not about the actions that need to be changed but about the labels.

Jeri and Robert came in arguing about whether or not she was alcoholic. Robert had come from an alcoholic family and was active in the Adult Children of Alcoholics movement. He was sure that Jeri was an alcoholic; she just as adamantly claimed she wasn't. As their therapist, Bill was startled to learn, when he asked for a video description of what Robert perceived as "alcoholic," that Jeri did not drink at all! Robert believed that the behavior Jeri showed was indicative of being on a "dry drunk." She was "grumpy" (spoke to him and the children in harsh and loud voice tones); she isolated herself (she would not talk to him for several days in a row); and she would try to control his behavior (she would criticize him for not keeping the yard up to the standards of the neighborhood). Once Bill heard a clear description of the actions that being on a dry drunk involved, it was simply a matter of negotiating changes in those behaviors. Jeri never did agree that she was alcoholic and Robert never changed his opinion that she was. Still, they were able to make enough changes so that they stopped arguing about the matter.

When your partner is acting in a way that may endanger the relationship, avoid labels and specify boundaries of acceptable and unacceptable actions. Be sure to be as specific and detailed as possible to prevent misunderstandings.

Bill and I both agreed that we would remain faithful to each other when we married. To Bill, this agreement meant that he would not get naked and have sex with anyone besides me. To me, it meant more. One time he called home from a workshop he was teaching and told me that he had a long dinner alone with a woman in a fancy restaurant. He was surprised when I became upset. I felt that Bill had violated our agreement about monogamy, or at least was headed in that direction. Bill's first reaction was, "Wait—we didn't have sex on the table. We just ate dinner." I explained that I thought it was an inappropriate context and too tempting an invitation to have dinner alone with a woman in a fancy restaurant. Given that Bill actually dislikes that kind of dinner anyway and that it troubled me, he agreed not to have dinner on the road alone with a woman. We also clarified that, for me, breakfast or lunch was not at all the same as a long dinner in a romantic setting, so I had no objection to Bill eating with a woman alone at those meals. The point is that we thought we had a clear agreement that we both understood, but we discovered that we each had different definitions of that packaged word *faithful*.

Although this example concerns a fairly minor incident, we often use the same principles in working with couples who are dealing with much more serious and frightening issues. Sometimes one partner has stepped out of bounds in a way that threatens the physical health, safety, or security of the other partner or the family. We have helped couples clarify a variety of issues, such as: any physical contact while one is angry is considered violence; or drinking *any* alcohol, however small an amount, and driving while the children are in the car is unsafe and unacceptable; or charging anything on a credit card is considered irresponsible. Make sure your action requests and action complaints are so clear that your partner does not have to guess about the limits of acceptable behavior.

> *Josh and Susan had frequently come to blows during their arguments. Josh complained that Susan was the first to get physical and that he only got physical in order to defend himself against Susan's violence. In a session with Pat they agreed that it was not acceptable for either of them to touch the other when they were angry and that this included shoving or poking in the chest with a finger. These boundaries had to be crystal clear to help them end the violence in their marriage. It still was hard for them to break their violent patterns, but after establishing the boundaries they were able to make changes by taking breaks when things started to escalate. One of them would go to the pay phone down the street to continue the discussion. They had to make a chart about whose turn it would be to go to the phone, otherwise that would have become the source of the next argument.*

Change the Patterns

The next option is to change your part of the patterns around violence or betrayal. Notice that we didn't say your *half* of the patterns. We're not suggesting that you are equally responsible for the problem patterns when your partner is violent or has an affair, just that you have *some* power to make *some* choices to do *some* things differently. It may be that you do something that is ten percent of the pattern. Your tiny part of the pattern might just be the self-blaming way you talk to your spouse about the difficulty. While it may be common for partners to blame themselves when their spouses are violent or have affairs, changing the conversation around the problem could be a beginning of a pattern change. Whenever you can change your actions or recognize a destructive pattern, you can begin to change the pattern.

In working with Josh and Susan, we next explored what hap-
pened around their violent episodes. Josh said that he could usu-
ally tell that Susan was about to get violent because she started
slamming things—banging pots and pans, slamming doors, and
stomping around the house. She agreed that these were warning
signs that preceded shoving and hitting Josh. They both agreed
that when these warning signs started, they would each go to
different parts of the house for thirty minutes. He had a shop in
the garage and he was comfortable with the idea of retreating
there; she had an office in a corner of the basement that would
work for her. They both thought that a half-hour break would
be sufficient time to interrupt the pattern. Changing this pattern
was enough to stop the violence between them.

Personal Power

Sometimes when there is an ongoing struggle over dangerous or
destructive behavior in a marriage, the love and concern that one
partner has for the other get lost. We suggest that when you con-
front your partner about destructive behavior, point out how important he or she is to you, how much love you share, and how
much you want the relationship to continue. It can have a powerful
impact to say, "I love you and I really need your help. I am so
worried about the financial problems that your gambling has caused
that I'm afraid to stay in this relationship. I want to find a way to
stay and feel secure. Please stop gambling or get some help." We
think of this approach as one of *using your personal power.* Inter-
ventions like this have been used successfully in the field of alcohol treatment for many years. When your partner is confronted
with love and concern instead of anger, he or she often responds
by changing the problem behavior. Pat tells the following story
to describe her personal experience of discovering the power of
love.

One time our then sixteen-year-old daughter, Angie, was in a situation that worried me. Angie had a friend, Katie, who had three older brothers with reputations as roughnecks and drinkers and a mom who was exhausted from being a single parent. When Angie was over at Katie's spending the night one Friday, I couldn't sleep because I was so worried about the situation. I did not want to forbid Angie from spending time with Katie, but I *was* concerned about Angie's safety. I decided to write a letter to Angie right there and then. It read:

Dear Angie,
   I couldn't sleep last night because I was so worried about you being over at Katie's house. I'm not sure it is safe there. I'm afraid something might happen to you while you are staying overnight. I love you very much, and from now on I would rather you have Katie stay overnight in our home instead.

Mom

Although it was the middle of the night, I drove over to Katie's house and left the letter on the windshield of Angie's car. I expected Angie to be furious, because she really chafed at being told what to do and was also easily embarrassed. But Angie so clearly felt the love and concern in my letter that she did not react with typical teenage indignation. In fact, the next night Angie even stayed home and watched television snuggled next to me (an unusual Saturday night activity for a newly licensed sixteen-year-old).

Lucy and Charles were close to breaking up over Charles's nightly stops at the bar with the guys after work. Lucy had already made it clear what she wanted: no driving after drinking. She came to us for help about what next to do with Charles. The relationship had become so strained that the word love *had not been mentioned in a long time. We suggested to Lucy that she*

*write a letter emphasizing her caring for Charles, her deep sad-
ness at what felt like losing him to alcohol, and her fear that, at
best, he was soon going to encounter the serious legal ramifica-
tions of drinking and driving. At worst, he might not be alive
much longer.*

*By coincidence, Charles had a car accident the week that she
gave him the letter. Although no one was seriously hurt, that
dose of reality, along with Lucy's loving plea, affected Charles.
He stopped drinking and came for therapy.*

This kind of strategy is in a special category of changing patterns.
When you have fallen into a pattern of rescuing (such as calling in
sick for a hungover spouse) or preaching and condemning, changing to an approach that emphasizes your love and caring can change
the relationship patterns. Of course, some people do not respond to
this loving approach; with those partners, it is time to use *consequences.*

Truth and Consequences

Many people object to the idea of giving their spouses consequences, thinking that consequences are only for children. But
sometimes adults become so out of control that consequences are
the only option. When adults regularly act in irresponsible and vol-
atile ways, consequences serve the same purpose as they would
with children—to encourage behavior change by highlighting personal responsibility and shifting the discomfort and pain of the mis-
behavior to the misbehaver.

Bill tells this story, which he calls "The Brick Wall," to illustrate
the importance of consequences.

I grew up in a large family of eight kids. My father died in the late
1970s. He had cancer and we all knew he was dying. To escape the
cold Nebraska winters, he came down to Arizona, where I was in

college. We had some great talks during his time in Arizona. He would tell me stories about the family and about life.

One day we started talking and he said, "You know, I learned one thing from raising eight kids." I said, "One thing?! I'd like to know what this one thing is. I work with families and kids all the time and plan to have a family of my own some day. Tell me about it."

He said, "Well, what I have learned is that the way kids learn about the world is by running into brick walls." "What does that mean?" I asked. thoroughly puzzled.

"When you're raising your kids," he said, "you see when they're about to make a mistake. Maybe they've gotten in with the wrong crowd of friends, or they're messing around in school and not doing very well, or they're getting into drugs or alcohol or delinquent behavior. Some of you kids have gotten into romances in which I knew you were going to get hurt. You watch your kids heading for some sort of trouble in the future as if they are riding a motorcycle towards a brick wall. You as a parent feel this tremendous need to stop them from hitting the brick wall.

"With the first two of you guys, I stood in front of the brick wall yelling, 'Look, stupid, you're heading for a brick wall! You're making a big mistake, you're messing up your life and you ought to turn around!' Of course, they would *speed up* on their motorcycle when I gave that lecture, then they'd flip me a rude gesture and promptly hit the brick wall. What was really terrible was that I was standing in front of the brick wall and they'd hit me first.

"So after the first two, I got a little smarter and I'd stand back away when I gave my lecture. 'You're heading for a brick wall! You're making a big mistake, you ought to get your life together and stop messing around!' They'd speed up, give me the rude gesture, and hit the brick wall, but this time I wasn't standing between them and the brick wall. So that was a little better. They would make their mistakes, but I wouldn't get so caught up in their messes myself.

"After six kids, I got *a lot* smarter. By then, when I'd see them heading for the brick wall, riding their motorcycles, I'd calmly take my seat. They'd be going by and I'd say, 'Look I'm an old man. I've been around for a while and I think there is a brick wall ahead. I suggest you go in a different direction. But I've had enough kids to realize that you're probably going to think I'm full of it and don't know anything. So all I can say is, I think there is a brick wall ahead. This is a mistake, but you have to learn your own lessons.' And when I'd say it that way, the kids would usually slow down their motorcycles a little. I noticed that the rude gesture dropped out entirely. And . . . they still hit the brick wall."

My father said that after all those kids, he finally realized that this is just what kids do. They try to figure out what the world is about by hitting the brick wall. They learn that they are responsible for what they do and that there are consequences when they make mistakes. Some adults still haven't learned this lesson, so consequences become the brick wall for them. Consequences help them realize that they are responsible for their actions. There is a difference between *consequences* and *punishment*. Punishment is intended to reform a person's character or to inflict injury or hurt as revenge. That is not what you want to do with an out-of-control adult (or child). Our goal is to make sure your partner experiences the negative consequences of his or her actions instead of inflicting those destructive consequences on you.

The best way to deliver consequences is in a non-blaming, matter-of-fact manner. Consequences should be like gravity. If you choose to jump off the porch, gravity doesn't care if you've had a good day or a bad day; gravity doesn't care if you are impulsive and can't help jumping off porches; gravity doesn't know about your dysfunctional family; gravity doesn't concern itself with your jumping genes. It just takes you down—without malice and with utter consistency. You jump; down you go. So, like gravity, be consistent but not blaming or punishing.

Larry was an ambitious man. As part of his quest for success he and Jenny had moved from the West Coast to the Midwest for a career opportunity. The move took Jenny away from her family. As a full-time homemaker with two small children at home, Jenny had felt isolated in the year since they had moved, so she called home often. She complained that Larry would regularly not come home until 7:30 or 8:00 at night, leaving her feeling abandoned in the world of motherhood. He usually did not let her know he was going to be late, which added anger and frustration to her loneliness. Meanwhile, he was angry at her for running up such large long-distance phone bills, but she protested that she was terribly lonely and that he apparently was unwilling to do anything about it.

It seemed obvious to us that simple courtesy could guide Larry in keeping his word about when he would come home and to call if he was going to be late. They made an agreement that Larry would tell Jenny when he was going to be home. If Larry was five minutes late, Jenny could phone her family and talk until Larry came home. Larry agreed that he would not complain about any long-distance charges made while he was late arriving. Jenny also agreed not to talk long-distance more than thirty minutes a week, with the exception of holidays and birthdays, and aside from the time she talked blame-free when he was late.

Sometimes when people have come to see us, they are so upset that the first consequence they think of is, "Dump 'em!" We think of consequences as something that should escalate a bit at a time. Start small. As one of Pat's clients said, "Why use a sledgehammer to kill a fly on a coffee table?"

Bev fell madly in love with Jed. She had previously seen Pat for help through a difficult divorce and had now brought Jed to meet Pat for her pre-marital approval. Pat was hesitant to give it because Jed had been out of alcoholism treatment for only two months. Pat knew that there is only so much rationality someone in love will listen to, so after suggesting that Bev take it slow, she left Bev to decide for herself. Bev married Jed two months later.

Jed was a would-be country-western singer. Bev was a factory worker who had saved $30,000 from her years of working and frugal financial management. Jed convinced Bev to bankroll his demo tape and trips to Nashville. After a year of failure and frustration, Jed returned to drugs for escape. He began smoking twenty-five dollars' worth of marijuana a day. Bev became concerned and returned to therapy.

Pat suggested that Bev stop putting her money in their joint account (pun intended) since Jed was not working. He then resorted to selling household items for drug money. After much painful deliberation, Bev refused to let him live in her house, and even changed the locks, but she still hoped he would stop using drugs and that their marriage could be saved. Finally, Jed hit her during an argument and, a few days later, she discovered he was having an affair. That was the last straw (or rather, the last two straws). Bev divorced Jed. Later Pat asked if, in hindsight, Bev would have preferred Pat to have encouraged her to get divorced sooner. Bev replied, "No. It was important to give the marriage every chance and not give up too soon. I needed to know that I did everything I could to save the marriage."

Bev had begun by clarifying the limits; she had changed her pattern from one of mere discussion to action by withholding money for drugs and, when that consequence proved useless, having Jed move out. Finally, when his impulsive behaviors increased despite their living apart, the consequences escalated to ending the relationship.

As this story demonstrates, consequences do not always succeed in motivating behavior change. However, they *do* help establish that the person who is doing the destructive or dangerous behavior is accountable.

Another couple we worked with had more success with this approach.

> *Frank and Tammy had been married for twelve years. Frank was physically abusive throughout their relationship and Tammy was ready to leave, in spite of the financial hardship she knew she would endure with the two children. They had separated twice, and once the divorce process had gone as far as the day before their court date, but Frank had always talked Tammy into reconsidering the relationship. In our session, Tammy promised us that if Frank touched her again in anger, she would go through with the divorce without discussing it with him. Frank was finally convinced of Tammy's intention to divorce him if he ever got violent again. We heard from them a year after counseling ended; Frank had not been abusive since Tammy had clarified exactly what the final consequence would be.*

Consequences are especially crucial when it comes to issues of physical safety. When no other consequence has motivated change, you may have to end the relationship. We are very committed to saving marriages and rarely recommend divorce. We are also firmly committed to preventing and ending violence in relationships. If violence is an ongoing problem in your relationship, and the approaches we recommend do not stop it, we urge you to separate or divorce.

The analogy we use for hopeless relationships is one of playing ball. It's as if you throw the ball to your partner, but he or she makes no attempt to return it. Undaunted, you throw the ball again, hoping to get a response. But, again, the ball just falls to the ground. At some point you begin to realize that it's time to quit the game because the other team isn't playing! We can't tell you how long to keep throwing the ball if your partner isn't playing—if he or she continues to drink excessively, have affairs, behave violently, or lies compulsively—but at some point you will probably want to move on and find someone who *does* want to play ball with you.

KEY POINTS: DEALING WITH A DESTRUCTIVE PARTNER

♥ Clarify the boundaries by using action requests so both parties know what is and is not acceptable.

♥ Change the pattern around the destructive behavior.

♥ Use your personal power by couching your request in love and concern for your partner.

♥ Escalate consequences for a partner who is destructive.

♥ If you have exhausted other options, sever the relationship.

ACTION STEPS: CHANGING DESTRUCTIVE/DANGEROUS BEHAVIOR IN RELATIONSHIPS

⇨ If you have already talked to your partner about what the boundaries are between acceptable and unacceptable behaviors, try writing a letter. It can either be as objective as a contract or as subjective as a plea expressing your love.

⇨ If your partner still refuses to respond, start to change parts of the destructive pattern that you can affect. Remember that even if you succeed in changing these patterns, it doesn't mean that you caused them or are accountable for your partner's behavior.

⇨ Begin to apply consequences, increasing the severity of the consequences if necessary. In the last action step you changed your part of the pattern; in this step you put your energies into direct consequences.

⇨ If none of the previous suggestions work and you cannot see any opportunity that will soon lead to a change in the destructive behavior, then perhaps it is time to consider ending the relationship.

In the next chapter we talk about what to do if you or your partner has violated the trust or safety in the relationship, but has now stopped the behavior and is willing to play ball. The good news is that it *is* possible to heal the hurt and restore the relationship. One way to accomplish this healing is through the use of healing rituals. Stay tuned.

I'M GONNA WASH THAT MAN
RIGHT OUTTA MY HAIR!

Healing Rituals for Unfinished Business
and Reconnection

What if you have used the methods from the previous chapters and things still aren't going well in your relationship? Sometimes people are haunted by unfinished business from previous relationships or from earlier conflicts and betrayals in their current relationship. This chapter offers an action technique—transition rituals—for rapidly resolving such unfinished business and connection rituals that nourish a sense of continuity and stability in your relationship.

Sometimes your current relationship is haunted by events from the past. If you or your partner has experienced affairs, physical violence, betrayal, death of a family member or previous spouse, rejection, sexual abuse, or other such traumas, you may have some unfinished business to address. If the betrayal, violence, or trauma is still happening, we suggest using the methods we described in the last chapter. When these traumas are no longer happening but their effects linger, one way to move on is to create a ritual, another action method for change.

We are using ritual here to mean more than religious ceremonies. By ritual, we mean any set of actions that comes to mean something other than the actions themselves. Rituals are symbolic. Religious rituals are only one kind of ritual.

In working with couples, we typically use two kinds of rituals: *transition* and *connection* rituals. Rituals should be used only after all the preliminary work has been done to resolve the trauma: acknowledging the violation, making and keeping clear agreements, and making amends. We are not suggesting that if you find out about an affair on a Monday that you have a ritual on the following Friday. Several weeks or months may need to pass before you are ready to do a ritual. "We will serve no ritual before its time," is our motto. But when the time is right, a ritual can be valuable for exorcising those ghosts that haunt your relationship.

The first type of ritual involves ceremonies that are set apart from everyday life and used to mark transitions—*transition rituals.* Daily, weekly, monthly, or yearly activities that people regularly engage in (such as eating dinner together, reading the paper together on Sundays, or holiday celebrations) can be used as *connection rituals.* This type of ritual provides stability and connection in the midst of the constantly changing nature of life. In our work with couples we use rituals in both ways: to help partners move on when they are stuck in problem patterns and to restore or create activities that help them connect.

Symbols

Before you carry out your ritual, it is important to find a symbol that physically represents whatever is unfinished for you. The symbol should be a concrete object that you can hold in your hands and do something with, and it must represent either the problem (un-

finished business) or a person, situation, or inner experience related
to the problem.

> *One couple was haunted by the memory of the wife's de-*
> *ceased husband. Bea was constantly comparing her new husband*
> *with her previous husband. We suggested she go to a lapidary*
> *shop and select a particularly attractive rock to represent her pre-*
> *vious marriage. She carried the rock around with her until she*
> *felt ready to let it (and the previous marriage) go. That, com-*
> *bined with other specific changes, helped this couple resolve*
> *their conflicts.*

Existing Symbols

You may have an object that was physically associated with the
problem person or situation. When we asked one woman what
would be a good symbol of her estranged husband, she selected a
golf hat he had favored. Other examples of this type of symbol are
pillows that the person used, photographs, articles of clothing,
motel bills, or jewelry. If the exact object is no longer available, you
can buy an identical or similar object.

> *Dave and Janine had been separated for a year because of an*
> *affair Dave had had with a neighbor. Dave had given the neigh-*
> *bor a key chain as a gift, which he could not now retrieve. In*
> *order to end this painful time ceremonially, Dave purchased a*
> *clear plastic key chain that had the name of the other woman on*
> *it and gave it to Janine, who smashed it with a hammer. That felt*
> *pretty good, but she decided it wasn't quite enough. After driv-*
> *ing back and forth over it several times with her car (thus giving*
> *thorough expression to her rage), she finally felt the issue was*
> *resolved.*

If you don't possess or can't find an object associated with the
person or situation, create one. The very act of creating a symbolic
object can become part of the ritual.

Created Symbols

Created symbols can be made specifically for your ritual. Depending on your talents and sense of things, poems, letters, pictures, or sculptures of the situation or person may represent what you want to leave behind.

> *Although Barb had a loving relationship with a man she had been involved with for the past six months, she was depressed. She found herself brooding over her ex-husband and their marriage, which had ended in divorce several years ago. Her ex-husband had been physically brutal to her and the children, had often been drunk, and frequently unfaithful. Once when he was angry, he had even tried to run over her and the children with the car.*
>
> *We suggested that she draw a picture representing her marriage. She protested that she wasn't much of an artist, but we told her that her artwork would not be hanging in the Metropolitan Museum of Art. It was to help her get free from her past. She drew a spiral that had more and more negative events on it, as though the relationship had been a whirlpool that had sucked her and her children into its treacherous vortex. When she returned for the next session, we told her to burn it. She was disappointed that she had drawn it to such a normal scale. She said, "If I had known that you were going to ask me to burn it, I would have made it huge so that I could have had the satisfaction of watching it burn for a very long time!"*

If you have long-term unresolved issues, a continuous letter can be a particularly useful symbol. By *continuous,* we mean that every day you write a letter to or about the problem person or situation. This project can last for a week, a month, or longer. Your sense of what still needs to be expressed determines whether days, weeks, or months are necessary to complete the continuous letter. You could also create a special place to write your letter—perhaps a little shrine on which to place your symbolic object with lighted candles on either side. We suggest you limit the amount of time that you write, and choose a specific time each day or evening to write.

> *Jane and Will had been married for two years. This was a second marriage for both of them. Jane's divorce had been very bitter and they both agreed that her anger toward her former husband was affecting her in this marriage. She decided to sit in front of a picture of her ex-husband and write a letter to him for thirty minutes a day, for as many days as she needed in order to feel that her rage toward him was dissipated. After three weeks of writing, Jane felt better. Then we had Jane and Will create a ceremony during which they destroyed the letter and the picture as a symbol of excluding this old relationship from their marriage. Then they celebrated with a romantic picnic that represented the specialness of their relationship.*

KEY POINTS: SYMBOLS

♥ Symbols are concrete objects that represent a person, place, inner experience, or situation and can be used to exemplify unresolved areas in your life or your relationship.

♥ Symbols of your unresolved areas may already exist (a photo, a key chain, a shirt) or can be created by writing, drawing, sculpting, sewing, gathering/collecting items of nature, etc.

Transition Rituals

Transition rituals are special events that serve as marking points for a variety of life experiences: moving to a new stage in a relationship; symbolically including or excluding a significant person into or from your life or relationship; getting over a traumatic event that has been haunting you, your partner, or your relationship; helping you or your partner resolve unfinished grief.

Rites of Passage

In relationships that last for any amount of time, roles change. At first you may be lovers; then you may be partners who are both career oriented; next you might be parents together; and eventually you return to one another as lovers and close companions after the kids leave home. Rites of passage can help you acknowledge these challenging transitions and prepare psychologically and emotionally for new roles. Our culture recognizes this at times and provides rituals. The ritual of both partners attending childbirth classes can facilitate the transition to parenthood. Bar mitzvahs, bat mitzvahs, and confirmations help parents and children make the transition from the roles and expectations that were appropriate for childhood and adolescence to new ones that help prepare for adulthood. Weddings—with their showers, bachelor parties and receptions— are designed to facilitate the passage from single life and the family one grew up in to married life and the beginning of a new family. Sometimes, however, the role change that needed to happen didn't and you've gotten stuck. With couples, sometimes the roles that the ritual is designed to change is an old image or identity from a previous time in the relationship. Other times, it is the relationship identity itself that needs to change. After an affair, perhaps the old marriage has to die before the new one can be born. That is when deliberately designing and carrying out a rite of passage can help.

One couple was stuck in the roles of "fragile mental patient" and "protective spouse." Lucy had had a "nervous breakdown" several years before, during which time she had taken an enormous amount of medication. Lucy felt that she had recovered and was no longer the fragile creature she had been when she went through that difficult time. Jerry, her husband, however, still feared that any sort of conflict would precipitate a break- down and therefore he would not argue or discuss controversial issues with his wife. Lucy wanted Jerry to treat her as a normal woman.

In discussing this issue with them, we learned that they had a medicine cabinet full of empty prescription bottles—some so old that they were made of glass instead of today's plastic. The cou- ple had kept these just in case any of her symptoms returned. As part of the ritual to mark their transition out of their old mental patient and protector roles, they wrote down the prescription information and put it in a safety deposit box in a bank (away from their daily life). Then they put all the empty bottles in a chest and buried it in their backyard. When they returned to the house after this burial, Jerry deliberately picked an argument with Lucy. Carrying out this rite of passage helped the couple acknowledge a new stage of their relationship in which they both had more freedom to express emotions and resolve con- flicts.

To help you acknowledge new roles or move into new phases in your relationship, rites of passage are recommended. When you are having trouble incorporating new people (in-laws, friends, or chil- dren) into your relationship or leaving someone behind, it's time for a ritual of exclusion or inclusion.

Rituals of Inclusion and Exclusion

Rituals can be used to redefine the boundaries of a relationship— indicate who is and is not included in the relationship. Engagement and wedding celebrations given by family members are rituals of inclusion, saying in essence, "Welcome to the family; we accept and approve."

When we married we were keenly aware that our decision was

also creating a stepfamily. We felt it was important that the children be the primary people who "stood up for us" in our wedding. Each of the kids lit a candle to initiate the ceremony. By including the three children from Pat's first marriage, we were making a clear statement that parenting together was a part of our commitment to each other and that we were creating a new family group.

You can use rituals of exclusion to clarify new boundaries in your relationship. One husband and wife decided to write separate letters to the "other woman" after the husband's affair had ended, telling her of their renewed commitment to their marriage and asking her not to contact either of them. They mailed the letters in the same envelope and later burned copies of the letters as a way of marking the end of the matter.

You can create rituals of inclusion and exclusion in combination. Issuing a "press release" to the children informing them that they are barred from the bedroom after a certain time is an example of an exclusion ritual. Having the new stepparent read to the children every other night, alternating with the biological parent, can be a nice inclusion ritual. Exclusion and inclusion rituals can be especially important in a stepfamily, where a couple is trying to create a bond and at the same time establish workable limits with the children. Statisticians tell us that by the year 2000, half of all families will be stepfamilies, so creating rituals that help people move through these challenging and increasingly common transitions may be essential.

Rituals of Mourning and Leaving Behind

Rituals can help you grieve the loss of a loved one; they can also help you leave something or someone behind in order to get your relationship back on track. Perhaps you share a loss as a couple, through miscarriage, the death of a child, or the death of someone you both love. Perhaps the loss is personal to you or your partner. Rituals help express grief under any circumstances, but they are especially helpful if you feel stuck in the process, or if you are over the grief but somehow still feel the effects in your relationship.

> *Beth came into therapy reporting difficulty with her five-year-old daughter, Suzy. As she talked, it became clear that the problem had begun after she had lost a child at birth two years before. She had been anesthetized during the birth process and had not seen the badly deformed child. Her husband, Brandon, had been present at the birth and had had an opportunity to see the baby and grieve.*
>
> *Since there had been no funeral, we suggested a ceremony. Brandon had kept a journal of his feelings during this time of loss and was eager to participate in the ritual. The couple bought a doll, kept it for a week, and then had a burial in the backyard. (The ritual did not include Suzy, as we mutually decided that she was too young to understand the ritual and Beth and Brandon thought it was primarily Beth's issue that was influencing her reaction to Suzy's behavior.) The ritual gave Beth an opportunity to share her feelings of inadequacy for having given birth to a child who was so badly deformed. Brandon, who had felt more complete in having dealt with his loss, read from his journal as part of the ceremony. This ritual brought them closer together and helped them deal more effectively with Suzy's misbehavior.*

Unresolved and sustained grief over a person or event outside your marriage can affect your relationship. A parent's death can interfere with a marriage in two ways: the grieving spouse may become so absorbed with grief that he or she is inaccessible to the spouse or the grieving spouse may be disappointed at the other's lack of support. If you find yourself in the awkward situation of not knowing what to say or do with a grieving partner, creating a ceremony can give you something concrete to do. The first step is to use the methods we gave you in the section on action requests in Chapter 2: ask your partner to tell you what he or she needs to help him or her through the grieving process. Perhaps the only request you receive will be to run interference with the children. If you are the one who is grieving, tell your partner what *you* need.

Steve and Ellen came to therapy for communication difficulties, disagreements over raising the children, and the desire for more closeness. In passing, Steve mentioned his annoyance that Ellen refused to throw away any of her deceased mother's belongings, even though it had been years since her death. After the couple's other conflicts were resolved, Ellen asked for a session alone. She reported that although her mother had died three years ago, she still felt that her mother was watching her and judging everything she did.

We asked Ellen to bring in three of her mother's less expensive possessions. She brought in a kitchen utensil, an iron, and a box of saving stamps from a now defunct company. Deciding that the saving stamps were a perfect symbol, we assigned her the task of carrying around the box of stamps for a week, telling her to keep it with her every minute. Even if she went to the bathroom in the middle of the night, she was to carry the box with her. At the end of the week, she was to dispose of the box.

Ellen did the assignment and found that it helped. She said that she had thought the ritual was silly, but that she had done it. After she had finished carrying the box around for a week, she had sent it to Wyoming, to be put in the basement of her mother's house, which Ellen still owned. After she had sent it off, she no longer felt that her mother was watching her. To the delight of her husband, she finally got around to getting rid of most of her mother's things.

Designing a ritual to symbolize the end of an event—reconciliation after an affair, the end of drinking as a disruption to the relationship, the end of in-law problems—can help you put the past behind you so that you can move on in your relationship.

Linda didn't really like her life. She was single and lonely, unhappy in her job. She had health problems and was overweight. One day at the supermarket, a man approached her and started a conversation. Observing her picking out a cantaloupe, he commented, "There's nothing better than cantaloupe and ice cream." She quietly agreed and moved on quickly. But the man casually followed her through the store. At first she was a bit annoyed and scared, but he was so charming that after a while she began to talk with him. Near the end of the shopping trip, he asked her to go to the park and eat some ice cream and cantaloupe with him. She agreed.

During their impromptu picnic, Dan found out that Linda was a teacher. He told her that he really liked teachers "with a bit of meat on their bones" and that he was very attracted to her. She was flattered. He asked her out on a date. She agreed, still not sure of him, but intrigued and excited. Perhaps her life would take a turn for the better, she thought.

The next few months were blissful. Dan turned out to be quite romantic, bringing her flowers, calling daily, writing her love poems. He was a successful businessman who made over $100,000 per year, he told her. They ended up falling in love and soon were having sex.

Then a few troubling signs began to surface. Dan refused to give Linda his home phone number or his address. He told her that he liked his privacy, and if she needed to call, she could call him on his cellular phone, which he kept in his truck. He started telling her his fantasies about having sex with her and another woman. He lied about little things on occasion. Still, aside from these minor complaints, the relationship was going well. She was happy for the first time in her life. Friends and co-workers told her that she was blossoming. She began to talk to Dan about getting married and he seemed eager at the prospect.

One day, Linda happened to mention Dan's name to a neighbor who, in their casual conversation, asked if Dan's wife still worked at the telemarketing firm. Linda was stunned and *thought the neighbor must have gotten Dan confused with someone else. But when she investigated, she found out that Dan was indeed married and even had a teenage daughter. When she confronted Dan with her discoveries, he became enraged at her "snooping." Later, he came to her house, confronted her, and, when she stood her ground, raped her anally. She pressed charges and, after a lengthy legal ordeal, Dan was tried and received a probationary sentence. (The district attorney felt that a jury was not going to be very sympathetic to a victim who had been dating a married man.)*

It had been well over a year since the court date, but Linda was still upset. She avoided people and was fearful of any man who showed an interest in her. She felt dirty, she said, especially her hair. Dan had admired her strawberry-blond hair and had once given her a very sensual shampoo. When she came for counseling with Pat, Pat kept thinking about the song from the musical South Pacific: *"I'm Gonna Wash That Man Right Outta My Hair." With that start, Pat and Linda designed a ceremony in which Linda wrote Dan a letter expressing all her feelings of being deceived, violated, and abandoned. She then burned the letter and washed her hair over and over again, listening to the song, until she felt she had washed Dan right out of her life. A few months later she wrote Pat to let her know she had started dating again and that Dan's memory no longer dominated her.*

This doesn't mean that you can instantly manufacture healing by quickly having a ceremony. Be sure that you have done enough talking and forgiving before you create a ritual. If you go through a ceremony to mark the end of an affair before you both feel certain that it is over and not going to happen again, then the ceremony will not bring a sense of closure and a new beginning. Similarly, if the ceremony is held too far after the appropriate time, then it will have little meaning for you. Timing is an important factor in determining the potency of the ritual.

Sharon and Rod were both career officers in the military. They had been separated for a year. During this time Sharon had told Rod that she wanted a divorce and then, because Rod said he did not want a divorce, she had come to therapy to consider the possibility of salvaging the marriage. Sharon had felt unsupported in the marriage and had had repeated affairs. Rod had been faithful but was not good at closeness and support. Through therapy, Sharon decided that she would work on the marriage again and she and Rod were reunited. During the time they were in therapy, Sharon found out that Rod had had a short affair with a married woman when he thought that his marriage with Sharon was over. Since they had both violated the marriage, they burned letters from the married woman and some things from Sharon's past and recommitted themselves to their marital vows. This ritual was followed by champagne and lovemaking. Sharon and Rod told us that they felt close to each other for the first time in their marriage and that they could never have experienced the much needed intimacy without having admitted their infidelities and created a ritual to leave the painful past behind.

Perhaps your marriage has so many problems that you would not even know in which area to create a ritual. If you and your partner have had a long history of painful interactions and yet you still want to try to make the relationship work, make some major changes and then have a funeral for the old marriage. It doesn't mean that you are divorcing. It means that you are giving the marriage a much deserved decent burial in the hopes that something new can rise from the ashes.

Randy and Grace had been through a horrible time in their relationship when they came to see Pat. Randy had had an affair four years earlier and Grace had just had an affair with Randy's close friend. To make matters worse, Randy had raped Grace

when he found out about her affair. At the time they came to
Pat, Randy had been living in an apartment for six months, away
from Grace and the children. Randy seemed to be using a hard-
sell technique with Grace, so Pat worked at ensuring that Grace's
point of view was heard and acknowledged. The first session of
marital therapy was spent discussing whether or not they were
going to make any attempt the save this badly deteriorated relationship. Grace was nearly convinced that the marriage was un-
salvageable, since things had been so awful. But, they did have
two children, a sixteen-year history, and Randy seemed motivated. He had been attending an abusers group at the YWCA
and had acknowledged his responsibility for raping Grace. They
both knew it would not be easy to go through a divorce, so even
Grace had some ambivalence about ending the marriage. Pat
agreed that their marriage was in very bad shape, in a coma at
least, if not D.O.A. The sexual violence was way beyond what
Pat could imagine tolerating in a marriage.

The couple mentioned that, even though they were separated, they were going on a trip with the children to visit rela-
tives in a large city. They both agreed that no matter what
happened to the marriage, they wanted to take this trip. Pat suggested that they could use the trip to let go of the old relationship
by creating a burial for the old marriage, then decide if they
wanted to start to work on building a new relationship. They
both liked the idea of a funeral for the old marriage.

Pat suggested that they each write a history of the marriage.
They were to write it over the course of the next week, taking
some time each day. When they went on their trip, they were to
take their marriage chronicles with them. On the trip they were
to burn the histories and take the ashes to a chapel in the city
they were visiting. Randy and Grace were to sit there in silence
for a half-hour contemplating what to do about the relationship.
Pat pointed out that it might be a challenge for Randy to sit
quietly in the chapel and resist trying to persuade Grace to stay in
the marriage, but he promised. (His keeping his word, Pat

*thought, might be particularly important, if Grace were going to
begin to rebuild any trust in him.) After their time at the chapel,
they were to find some proper place to dispose of the ashes and
discuss what they wanted to do next.*

*Pat saw them a month later. They had decided that they
would at least give the relationship four more months and that
Randy would move back into the house during those months.
Because of the rape, Grace insisted that Randy not touch her and
not come into her bedroom. Pat thought it was a good idea to
move this slowly, since it would likely take time to recover from
that level of violation. As of this writing they are still in the
process of working on the relationship. Pat feels it could go either way but Randy and Grace both have the sense that they
have left a large part of their painful past behind.*

Celebration

When we first started using these techniques with couples, we did
not pay much attention to how they ended their rituals. But we
have learned from them that it is important to create some kind of
transition from the ritual itself back into everyday life. Often this
transition takes the form of a celebration. You might go out for a
special dinner or take a weekend trip to highlight and reflect on the
changes you've just made as a couple. You could include others in
your celebration or you may want to keep it private. You can even
include friends or family in your celebration but not tell them that
they are part of the end of your ritual. It is up to you. Many issues
around which people create rituals (such as getting over an affair)
are extremely private.

If you have created a ritual to mark an important change in your
relationship, then bring it to a satisfactory completion by celebrating your triumph in a way that reorients you to everyday life. We
learned this from a Native-American woman at one of our seminars. She told us that in her culture, when someone has completed

an important ritual, he or she goes away for a time and then is welcomed back into the tribe and everyday life with a celebration. When you do something as odd as throwing a rock attached to a letter to your ex-spouse in the river, shouldn't you do something as normal as going out with friends to eat afterwards?

KEY POINTS: TRANSITION RITUALS

♥ Transition rituals are used to help you move on when you are stuck in problem patterns. They involve taking actions that symbolize change.

♥ There are three kinds of transition rituals: rites of passage, rituals of inclusion and exclusion, and rituals of mourning and leaving behind.

♥ Rites of passage are ceremonies that help you make the transition from one role that no longer serves you to another more fitting role.

♥ Rituals of inclusion and exclusion involve doing something that signals to yourself, your partner, and others that you are either including someone in your life or severing a relationship.

♥ Rituals of mourning and leaving behind are actions that help you express and resolve unfinished grief.

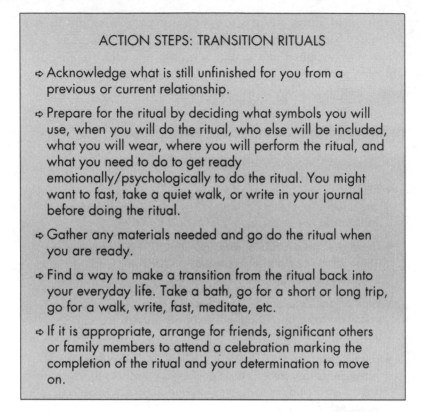

ACTION STEPS: TRANSITION RITUALS

⇨ Acknowledge what is still unfinished for you from a previous or current relationship.

⇨ Prepare for the ritual by deciding what symbols you will use, when you will do the ritual, who else will be included, what you will wear, where you will perform the ritual, and what you need to do to get ready emotionally/psychologically to do the ritual. You might want to fast, take a quiet walk, or write in your journal before doing the ritual.

⇨ Gather any materials needed and go do the ritual when you are ready.

⇨ Find a way to make a transition from the ritual back into your everyday life. Take a bath, go for a short or long trip, go for a walk, write, fast, meditate, etc.

⇨ If it is appropriate, arrange for friends, significant others or family members to attend a celebration marking the completion of the ritual and your determination to move on.

Connection Rituals

Often couples have become so involved in either their children's lives or their own careers that their relationships suffer in the process. The increasing number of dual-career relationships has made it even more challenging for couples to preserve a sense of intimate connection with one another. Couples must share regular times and activities that give them a feeling of connection, vitality, and stability. Connection rituals are regularly repeated activities—meals, attending church, birthday celebrations, bowling nights—that strengthen a couple's relationship. The importance of connection rituals was shown by research with alcoholic families. Jane Jacobs and Steve Wolin of George Washington University found that the disruption of family rituals (such as dinners, vacations, and holidays) by the alcoholic member increased the impact of the problems experienced by family members. When the rituals were kept intact, the family was less likely to take on an identity as an alcoholic family and the children were less likely to continue the alcoholism in the next generation. Connection rituals provide a kind of relationship "glue" that helps couples and families stay together through difficult times.

Friends of ours told us a charming story. When they were dating, Frank used to cook dinner for Sandy regularly at his house. After dinner, they would do the dishes together; he would wash and she would dry. They both enjoyed the after-dinner ritual of cleaning up and had some of their best conversations during that time. After several dates Sandy noticed that Frank's kitchen had a dishwasher. She assumed it was broken and teased him about being a procrastinator for not getting it fixed. He told her that it wasn't broken. "Why did we wash all those dishes by hand then?" she asked in amazement. "The first night," Frank explained, "there were so few dishes that I thought it would be a waste to use the dishwasher. Then I realized that I enjoyed doing the dishes with you so much, I didn't tell you about the dishwasher for fear it would rob us of that special time." Washing dishes by hand had become a connection ritual for this couple, which they use to this day.

One couple we worked with had five children, all involved in time-consuming activities such as paper routes, swim team, and gymnastics. Their "couple time" had become eroded by family activities. Each had become convinced that the other partner no longer had any interest in him or her. Prior to marital therapy, Jennifer had drowned her sorrows with alcohol, developing an alcohol problem that was resolved by inpatient treatment before we met them. Jim had immersed himself in his work. An important part of their healing was the simple act of making time for just the two of them. Specifically, they decided to let the children know that after 10:00 P.M. their bedroom was off limits by placing a closed sign on their door each night at that time. The couple also made a commitment to turn off the TV at 10:00 P.M. That commitment was backed up by placing their television power plug into a timer that automatically turned off at that time. They made a habit of talking for half an hour when the TV went off each night. Finally, they also arranged to go out socially without the kids once a week.

Arranging for regular times to connect provides a sense of continuity to a couple's life. Pat was giving a speech about communication and mentioned the importance of time alone for couples. A woman from the audience came up to Pat afterwards and said, "My husband and I have been married for twenty-five years and we have three grown children. Every Thursday night for these past twenty-five years, we have gone out alone for dinner. We have a good marriage and Thursdays are the main reason."

One of our favorite connection rituals is lying in bed discussing our day's activities every evening after the kids have gone to sleep. We also have monthly and yearly connection rituals. We were married on the 23rd of February, so we take the 23rd of each month off work and spend it together, and we take a week's vacation in February to celebrate our anniversary.

Remember our discussion about reinstating solution patterns that have worked for you earlier in your relationship? You may have had some previous rituals that have gone by the wayside that you could resurrect and restore as habits of connection. If not, it's time to develop some.

Another source of ideas for connection rituals can be other couples. What do friends of your do to renew their connection with one another? What did your parents do to connect? Because we talk to many couples about their relationships, we have gotten some great connection ritual ideas from others. Pat gets a back rub almost every night since we heard from friends of ours that that was their nightly ritual of reconnection. We both enjoy the touch and Pat, who gets pretty tense running a business, writing, doing a radio show, and keeping up with household and family activities, mellows quickly after a few minutes of massage.

KEY POINTS: CONNECTION RITUALS

♥ Connection rituals are regular (daily, weekly, monthly, seasonally, yearly) activities that can be used to reinforce your connection to one another.

♥ You may have had some connection rituals in the past that have gone by the wayside due to life changes (children, a career change, aging, financial changes). Sometimes you can reinstate them, but other times you may need to create new rituals that fit better with your current situation.

ACTION STEPS: CONNECTION RITUALS

⇨ Recall some regular habit or activity from earlier in your relationship that helped connect you to your partner. Talk to your partner about reestablishing that pattern or some variation of it that would fit better with your current circumstances.

⇨ Make a regular (daily, weekly, seasonally, yearly) habit of doing the activity. You may need to schedule it until it becomes habitual.

⇨ Observe and investigate other people's marriages. What regular habits of connecting, spending time together, or getting closer do they use? Would any of those, or a variation on any of those, work for you? Experiment with any ideas from your investigation that intrigue you.

YOU MEAN YOU CAN TALK DURING THIS?

Intimacy and Sex

Because so many of the couples we see in therapy have problems in the areas of sex and intimacy, here we show how you can apply the methods from the previous chapters to these crucial areas. This chapter offers action plans for developing intimate relationships. The sex section will show you how to solve your sexual problems and create great sex.

We once read a story in a letter to a newspaper advice columnist. The woman wrote that she had been standing at her usual bus stop in the big city in which she worked one miserable, rainy night. There must have been a problem with the busses, because her bus didn't arrive at its usual time, nor did the next one.

Her office building was locked and she was getting colder and more miserable, when a car pulled up and stopped. A man rolled down the window to tell her that he didn't usually offer rides to strangers, but that she looked so miserable, he couldn't pass her by that night. He told her he was going straight up the avenue for quite a way and he would be glad to give her a ride. He assured her that he wasn't a rapist or serial killer, just a Good Samaritan. She hesitated. Normally, she would never accept a ride from a stranger, but she was miserably cold and he seemed nice, so she nervously decided to get in the car.

Once inside, they started a pleasant conversation. By the time they arrived in front of her apartment building, they were both reluctant to end the conversation, so they sat in the car at the curb talking, until finally, throwing caution to the wind, she decided to invite him up to her apartment for dinner. He accepted and they ordered dinner to be delivered from a restaurant down the street. They had a great dinner, laughing and talking like old friends. She would never have imagined doing anything like this—it was so out of character for her, but somehow it seemed right. When it came time for after-dinner drinks, they began to kiss. One thing led to another and they ended up making mad, passionate love. He spent the night and they had fabulous sex several more times. After they kissed good-bye in the morning and he had left, she realized she was so caught up in the magic of the evening, she had forgotten to learn his last name. She was forlorn. She waited several days and he still hadn't called her or dropped by. She wrote asking for advice from the columnist. "What should I do?" she wrote. The columnist's answer was short and sweet: "Pray for rain!"

Many couples are like this woman. They are praying for rain or some similar accident of fate to provide the opportunity for the intimacy or passion they long for. In this chapter, we'll provide active ways to create closeness and passion in your relationship; in other words, you'll learn to create your own rain.

What Does Intimacy Look Like?

Intimacy is one of those packaged words we mentioned earlier. What does intimacy mean to you? Is it talking . . . snuggling in bed . . . discussing your day . . . or just being near each other and not talking? To create intimacy, one of the first things that you need to do is clarify what intimacy means to you and your partner. What *actions* do you want when you ask for more intimacy or closeness?

There are no dictionaries that can give us a universal definition of intimacy. Intimacy is different for different people. One woman said that she felt closest to her husband when taking a walk with him. A man said that he felt closest to his wife when they were sitting next to one another, holding hands and watching television. Another man said that having his wife read to him at night felt intimate. So, step one is getting a videotalk description of intimacy and asking your partner to do more intimacy-creating actions.

Removing the Barriers to Intimacy (One Brick at a Time)

If you and your partner do not feel intimate, it may be because things happen that keep you emotionally distant. Recurring problems can become a barrier to intimacy. The tools we have given you in the previous chapters (using action complaints and requests, changing problem patterns, and doing healing rituals) are designed to quickly and easily remove those barriers and create the kind of environment in which intimacy can flourish.

> *Marlis and James could never seem to get in sync with each other. After a day full of little conflicts, James' impulse was to have sex; he thought that would bring them together. Marlis felt it was impossible for them to be close enough for sex when they had been sniping at each other all day. After struggling with this difference for some time, Marlis was getting more and more turned off sexually. They decided that they would shelve the issue of having sex, since it was a point of contention, and look for other ways to build an intimate relationship. We asked them to think about the friends they had outside the relationship. What* actions *created those friendships? Marlis' friend Jeannie would ask Marlis about her day, listen to her concerns, and fre-*

*quently tell Marlis about the qualities she admired in her. James'
friend Pete would do things with him—like attending sports
events, working on projects (such as building a deck), and discussing their work. Soon both James and Marlis began making
efforts to act with each other as their friends did with them. With
this improvement and their learning to use videotalk when they
had conflicts, they were able to experience a new feeling of
closeness that helped restore their sexual relationship.*

One of the common barriers to intimacy is what we call the *wall
of evaluation,* which is built when either partner is getting the message from the other that he or she is somehow bad or wrong. Negative evaluation from a partner can be like a wall that you bump into
when you start to get close to one another. The bricks in this wall
might be made of constant little criticisms, of frequent judgmental
looks, expectations of perfectionism, or a refusal to admit mistakes.
Some time ago we read a story that illustrates this point well.

A wife was trying to parallel park the car in a fairly tight spot. All
the while, her husband kept up a steady stream of critical comments. Finally, exasperated, she stopped the car and told him that,
since he obviously thought he could do a better job than she was
doing, perhaps he'd like to switch places with her and do it himself.
He agreed and got in the driver's seat, where, in a huff, he proceeded to back the car up over the curb. When the car stopped
bouncing, the man turned to his wife and said, "Look what you
made me do!" There's no way to be right when confronted with
this kind of reaction—you are always wrong.

If you are giving your partner that sense of being wrong or bad,
find out which of your actions contribute to his or her getting that
message and start changing those patterns. If your partner regularly
communicates that you are wrong, talk to him or her about those
actions that feel to you like criticism or negative evaluation. Then
you can start to dismantle that wall of evaluation one brick at a
time.

How Does Your Intimacy Garden Grow?

Other couples, though not generally judgmental, neglect the on-going maintenance of the closeness in their relationship. They assume that, once they have developed a sense of intimacy, they can count on it being there in the future. That's like planting a garden and then never weeding or watering it. It may survive, but usually a garden needs regular tending to keep it growing the way you want it to.

We talked about finding your solution patterns in Chapter 3. Some of those solution patterns are actions that create or maintain your sense of intimacy with one another. If you've had trouble defining intimacy or finding a description of what intimacy would look like to you, you can think back to what you *have* done when you were intimate in the past.

Elizabeth and Roger had been married for twelve years. They had time-consuming careers and two young children (five and seven years old). They both complained that they didn't feel close and, even though they weren't approaching divorce, they knew things were deteriorating between them. It was difficult for them to recall what used to happen when they had been close. But searching in the dusty recesses of their memories, they finally remembered lying in bed and making love until mid-morning as being a wonderfully intimate time. Unfortunately, this memory initially made them feel even more discouraged, for it occurred PCT (pre-children time), they told us. They could not imagine hours of carefree lovemaking with the kids in the house. But they did come up with two ideas. One was to arrange for the kids to leave them alone until 10 A.M. on Saturday mornings. The kids agreed to get their own breakfast and watch cartoons. The second idea was to take advantage of the weekend package deal at a local hotel, scheduling a sitter to stay overnight with the children. Both of these arrangements helped renew their sense of connection and intimacy.

The Martian's Guide to Intimacy

Some couples don't have a clue as to what is missing in their relationship or what intimacy looks like to either one of them. After
seeing so many couples in marriage counseling over the years, we
have noticed some general principles used by most couples who are
intimate. We call this "The Martian's Guide to Intimacy" because
it answers the question: What would a Martian who came to Earth
to study intimate Earthlings find them *doing?*

First, our Martian anthropologist would notice that *people who are
intimate spend time together.* Unfortunately, the luxury of time to talk
and interact is often more available at work than at home.

> *Maxine and Terry, two women who were in a long-term
> committed relationship, came for counseling complaining that
> the spark seemed to have gone out of their relationship. They
> were raising two children together, ages eight and ten. When we
> asked them about their patterns of intimacy, we found out that
> they had none. It wasn't surprising. They worked opposite shifts.
> Maxine worked during the day and once she arrived home, the
> couple had just enough time to get the kids and themselves fed
> before Terry went off to work in her night-shift job. Weekends
> were not much better, as they spent what little time they had
> together doing household chores and errands or running the kids
> to music lessons and sports events. With our help, they made a
> commitment to get a sitter for Saturday nights so that they could
> go out on dates. They also decided to go for walks together on
> Sunday mornings, leaving the kids at a neighbor's house for an
> hour or so. Even with this small amount of time together, they
> were able to rekindle the spark they thought had gone out of
> their love life.*

Second, our Martian would notice that *people who are intimate talk
about vulnerable feelings, hopes, and dreams.* We've noticed that men
typically do not share their vulnerable feelings (such as fear, hurt, or

embarrassment) as readily as women do. Many men seem to specialize in showing only one emotion: anger. If you are a man, we have an experiment for you. Try saying one thing a week about something that has worried you, frightened you, or hurt you that week. If your partner responds well, maybe you should make a habit of telling her or him your vulnerable feelings.

Bill once had an experience that brought home to him the power of vulnerability. I had been working in a counseling center for a number of years and was leaving the job. There was another counselor at the center, John, whom I had never liked. I felt John was a lousy therapist who shouldn't be allowed to counsel people. I even made fun of John behind his back, imitating his slow speech, although I am not in the habit of ridiculing people. In spite of my adverse feelings, John regularly sought out my company, and I would always make excuses in an attempt to avoid interacting with him. I would do almost anything, even dreaded paperwork, to avoid this guy.

The last week I was at the center, John came into my office and planted himself firmly in a chair. He then proceeded to tell me how much he admired me, because I appeared to be so confident and competent. John confessed that he always felt scared and incompetent at work, and that he had wanted to spend time with me so that maybe some of my confidence and skills would "rub off" on him. John said he regretted that we hadn't gotten to know each other better. As I listened to this honest expression of feeling, my own feelings changed. No longer able to depersonalize John, I felt a sense of compassion for him. I even began to *like* John as our conversation continued. John's honest vulnerability had evoked a feeling of closeness in me. Vulnerability can elicit closeness, even in the unwilling.

Talking about vulnerable feelings can be a good litmus test of the potential for intimacy in a relationship. How does your partner (or potential partner) react to your intimate admissions? If you revealed that you had always wanted to be a missionary and your partner snorted, "You! Are you kidding?" that might be a good hint that he or she is not a good candidate for intimacy. *Vulnerability* means just that—the person who is doing the revealing is vulnerable to being hurt—so take care to respond nonjudgmentally when your partner is so exposed.

The third observation that our Martian anthropologist would make is that *people who are intimate touch each other a fair amount.* Maybe they hug or hold hands; maybe they put their arms around each other and sit close enough so that their bodies touch. If the Martian gains access to bedrooms, it will also observe sexual touching.

We have used "The Martian's Guide" principles to "prime the pump" of intimacy with some couples.

When Carole and Dennis sought Pat's help for their marriage, there had been such a long spell of emotional distance that Pat could almost hear a wind whistling across the wasteland of their relationship. In her mind she kept seeing dust and tumbleweed as the couple talked about their life together. They didn't talk much—in fact, they didn't seem to have enough emotional contact to even have an argument. They wondered if they still loved one another. Pat first suggested Martian step number one: time together. Then she focused on helping them start to do intimacy-creating behaviors.

Since they had not had sex for six months, Pat started with simple affectionate touching (another one of the Martian steps) by suggesting they give each other foot and hand massages. Creating a non-threatening context for touching was particularly helpful for Dennis, because he said that he had felt closest in the past when he had had physical contact with Carole.

After these initial changes had created positive feelings, Pat gave them the assignment of interviewing each other as though they were going to write one another's biographies. We have noticed that one of the ways people first get close is by sharing stories about each other's pasts. This is also one way to start talking about hopes and vulnerabilities.

After a few sessions Carole and Dennis felt closer and started to have sex again. Feeling that they had gotten the hang of creating intimacy with each other, they decided they would continue on their own. It happened that Pat ran into them a few years later and they happily told her that they had continued to enjoy intimate feelings with each other. As so often happens, once the ball is rolling in the right direction, it keeps rolling.

The next observation our Martian scientist would make is that *intimacy is usually different for men and women.* For women, intimacy involves discussing the nature of your relationship, your intentions in the relationship, and your feelings of affection for the other person. For men, no discussion is necessary.

Bill and I well portray these differences in our relationship. Bill has a close male friend. Bill has noticed that, although this friendship is probably the closest relationship he has outside his family, he and his friend rarely, if ever, talk about their relationship. Their closeness is just assumed. *If I'm doing things with you, then I obviously like you. If we are friends for years and have spent lots of time together, we are close friends.* This approach definitely does not work with me. If Bill does not talk with me about our relationship, I worry that there is something wrong. This difference is not unique to our relationship. Perhaps this disparity is a result of the way men are socialized. Whatever the reason, men rarely discuss their relationships with their "best buddies." Women, we think our Martian would notice, generally discuss their relationships with their intimates.

This is not to say that one way is right and one way is wrong. Blaming each other or assuming, "My way is the only true way to do intimacy," only blocks intimacy. It is important for Bill to know what my definition of intimacy is and learn to do more of that, even when it is not his natural inclination. It is equally important for me to learn that when Bill is spending time with me, though not talking directly about our relationship, he is probably indicating that he cares very much for me and is feeling close to me. Finding a balance between these two ways of doing intimacy usually takes time to stabilize and fine-tune, but it is well worth the effort.

One other action that we think our Martian friend would observe is that people who are intimate *do thoughtful actions for each other—grants of daily loving behaviors.* We call these *grants,* not loans, because loans need to be paid back, but grants are given freely. A grant has no contingencies. "I'll cook tonight, if you cook tomorrow night" is not a grant. Things like bringing coffee to your spouse in bed, going outside to get the paper for him or her, getting something repaired that your partner was supposed to handle— these are the little grants of kindness that a Martian would observe when studying intimate couples.

KEY POINTS: GENERAL CHARACTERISTICS OF INTIMACY

♥ Spending time together.

♥ Talking about vulnerable feelings, memories, hopes, and dreams.

♥ Affectionate touching.

♥ Discussing the relationship (or not).

♥ Grants of daily loving behaviors.

ACTION STEPS: INTIMACY

⇨ Tell your partner what intimacy looks like and sounds like to you. Find out the same information from him or her. Remember to use videotalk to make sure that each of you understands specifically what constitutes intimate behavior.

⇨ Ask your partner to fill in the blank in the following sentence. "I have felt closest to you when you _____ [description of some action you have done]."

⇨ Give your partner the same information. "I have felt closest to you when you _____ [description of some action your partner has done]."

⇨ Ask your partner to tell you about a time when he or she felt distant from you and what you did or said that contributed to the distancing. Listen without defending yourself or accusing your partner. Just receive the information and let it "soak in" for a while.

When you are having trouble in your sex life, often it is because there is a lack of intimacy in your overall communication. Once you have created more non-sexual intimacy, your sexual problems may also be resolved. However, if you are feeling intimate but your sex life is not all that you want it to be, the next section provides active ways to create a better sex life. Even if you don't have any sexual problems, you might want a tune-up or just a check-up in this area.

Sex Is a Bit Like Back-Scratching

If you have good communication, chances are you'll have good sex. Everything we have said about good communication in other relationship areas applies to creating a satisfying sexual life: tell your partner when he or she is doing something you do not like (sexual complaints); ask for what you want (sexual requests); and let your partner know when he or she is doing something you like (sexual praise).

One barrier to communicating clearly about sex arises because sex is so distorted in our culture. We don't even know what words to use for sexual communication. When discussing sexual matters, we use either street language or language that sounds like a medical school course ("Please place your digit upon my labia"). It is difficult for many couples to talk about what is going on "down there" (as they used to say in Bill's Catholic school days), but that is exactly what has to happen to have good sex. Somehow you have to convey what you like and what you don't like.

Sex is a bit like back-scratching. Nobody instinctively knows the best way to scratch *your* back, partly because only *you* can feel your sensations and partly because your back itches in different places at different times. If you ask someone to scratch your back, you'd probably be comfortable telling him or her, "Down just a little, over to the right, now down just a bit more. Ahhh, there, now harder, ohh, yeaah." Why don't we do this about sex?

> *In a counseling session once, the wife, Rhonda, finally revealed that her husband, Jeff, had been rubbing her clitoris very roughly since their first sexual encounter years ago. All this time, he had assumed that she was writhing in pleasure when she had actually been writhing in discomfort. (You've got to admit, it's sometimes hard to tell the difference from facial expressions during sex.) So Jeff kept it up longer. Rhonda was afraid her negative feedback would challenge his masculinity, so she had suffered in silence all those years. Once we helped Rhonda express her concerns without blaming or invalidating Jeff, he was able to learn to stimulate her in a way that brought her pleasure.*

Because so many of us feel shame around sexual matters, take care not to blame or invalidate your partner for his or her sexual experiences or interests. You each have the right to your values about sex. Don't give your partner the message that there is something wrong with him or her for not wanting what you want or for wanting something that you don't want.

> *Roy and Linda wanted different things in their sex life. Linda was content with the missionary position; Roy wanted Linda to perform oral sex on him. Linda's biggest fear, she said, was that the children might walk in the bedroom and see her doing this. Even after they got a lock for the bedroom door, however, she was still uncomfortable with oral sex. Roy began to call her a prude. She became defensive, thinking she had to justify why she didn't like oral sex in order to prove there was nothing wrong with her. She also knew that Roy wanted to explore entering her from behind. She had refused to do this, telling him she thought he was a "pervert" for wanting to do something "sick" like that.*
>
> *When they finally learned the simple idea of not judging or labeling each other, but just asking for what each wanted sexually, the logjam broke. At Roy's urging, Linda read a popular instruction book on sex and decided that although she still didn't want to do oral sex, she would be willing to experiment with a rear-entry position. She even discovered that she enjoyed this variation occasionally and soon added still other positions to their sexual repertoire. Roy was re-energized about their sex life and Linda discovered that she had orgasms more quickly and more often when she was on top during intercourse.*

The Pleasure Training Session (You Mean You Can Talk During This?)

Since many couples we see in counseling have never communicated clearly about what they want (and don't want) sexually, we have come up with a technique that provides a structure for doing just that. It's called the "pleasure training session." Set aside at least a half-hour for the session. Then start to touch and sexually stimulate your partner in any way that is acceptable to you and him or her. You might use your fingers, your hands, your tongue, a feather, your hair, your penis, or anything else you can come up with (pardon the pun). The person receiving the stimulation is to give feedback such as "harder . . . softer . . . move your tongue (fingers) slower (faster)."

Next, try two different sexual actions and ask your partner which one he or she likes better. (If it is too distracting to give comments during sex, wait until afterwards.) When it feels like the right time, switch roles of giver and receiver.

We once heard a joke about a woman who dated an optometrist. She had liked him, but the sex had driven her crazy. He kept asking, "Is it better like this . . . or like this? Like this . . . or like this?" If you've ever gotten an eye exam, you'll get this one; if not, oh well. That joke is no joke. In fact, it illustrates the essence of our pleasure training session. Keep asking questions as a way of getting to know your partner's preferences.

Pat is grateful to a woman from Bill's past, because this woman's openness ultimately contributed to Pat's fulfilling sexual relationship with Bill! Bill, blushing, tells this story.

I was raised Catholic, so there was not much talk or instruction about sex (except, as we mentioned before, vague admonitions about not touching yourself "down there"). In addition, I was very shy until I reached my late twenties. Consequently, neither I nor my first couple of sexual partners—all shy people—ever talked about sex during or after the act. Since they didn't talk, I never knew if they enjoyed what I did, if I was doing anything right or wrong, or even if they had orgasms. I assumed that they must have liked the sex a little, because they did seem to want to have sex again. I certainly never taught them what *I* did and didn't like.

Several years later, I began a relationship with a woman who was very open and assertive about sex. The first time we were sexual together, she started talking. She said things like "Put your hand here. . . . Touch it very lightly. . . . Yes, that's it. . . . Rub harder." I was in a state of shock. I thought to myself, *You mean people can talk during this?* Then she began to ask me things like "What do you like? . . . Does that feel good? . . . Should I do more of that?" I was even more startled, *You mean I have to talk during this, too?* It took some time, but eventually I started to talk more and more openly with her about what I liked and wanted her to do.

If you're one of those people who is too inhibited to say what you want out loud, we have come up with a special signal system to let your partner know what you like and don't like during sex. We call this the Hudson-O'Hanlon Squeeze Technique (as opposed to the more famous "Masters and Johnson Squeeze Technique"). The pleasure-receiver squeezes the pleasure-giver's *right* arm to signal, "I like that . . . do more of that," and squeezes the pleasure-giver's *left* arm to indicate wanting less of that kind of stimulation. (This technique is not recommended for dyslexics. It could really screw up your sex life. You'd better use moans for more and groans for less.)

Whether you use words, moans, groans, or squeezes during or after sex, we encourage you to dive in, so to speak, and initiate communication with your partner so that, at long last, you can teach each other what you like and don't like.

The Mix 'n' Match Sexual Menu

Perhaps you and your partner have communicated clearly about what you want and don't want in sex, but nevertheless find your-selves in a sexual rut. We have a simple suggestion for livening things up that involves creating a mix 'n' match menu of sexual behavior. The *doers* are any parts of the body that have muscles that can be used to initiate stimulation. The *doees* are the parts of the body that can receive stimulation. We suggest that you and your partner match items from column *A* with items from column *B*. It is like a Chinese restaurant menu—choose one "item" from each column. Perhaps you will connect the fingers and the mouth: You would like your partner to suck your fingers or you would like to suck theirs. Maybe you've never thought of that or you've thought about it but just not told your partner. The mix 'n' match menu provides another way for you to begin to communicate about your likes and dislikes and to become more creative in your sex life.

With couples who want to improve their sex life in counseling, Bill will sometimes write this menu on the blackboard in his office. He then asks each partner to match up two items. If neither of them speaks, due to fear or embarrassment, just to break the ice, Bill will pipe up cheerily, "Okay, how about tongue on anus, who likes that?" After we deal with that one, all the rest of them are easier, for some reason.

The Mix 'n' Match Sexual Menu	
A **Doers**	**B** **Doees**
Fingers	Mouth
Tongue	Clitoris
Mouth	Penis
Penis	Vagina
Vagina	Breast
Hand	Nipples
	Anus
	Skin

Remember that we are talking about *requests* here. As we said earlier, sometimes your partner will have objections to doing the requested actions. In sex, it is especially important to make sure you don't pressure your partner into doing something he or she does not want to do or make him or her feel weird or bad for not wanting to do what you want to do. So, if one of you draws a line between tongue and anus and the other is willing, fine. But if the other says "No way!" then move on to something that is comfortable for both of you. There are a lot of sexual choices available. Surely you'll be able to find some areas of agreement.

Pat met a woman who had attended the class that this is the basis of this book. They had a chance to drive together to a meeting and Pat asked the woman if there was anything that she had found particularly useful from the class. The woman seemed a little embarrassed when she said, "The Mix 'n' Match Sexual Menu." She said that she has been married for over fifteen years and that the menu provided her and her husband with an easy and fun way of reinvigorating their sex life.

The Ins and Outs, Ups and Downs, of Sexual Problems

There are a variety of sexual problems that people and couples develop. Some problems are purely medical or physical issues, of course, and we don't deal with those here. It is always a good idea to ask your doctor about any sexual problem you have in case there is a clearly physical basis for it. Some medications interfere with getting erections and lubricating properly, as can alcohol and nonprescription drugs. Changes in hormones as a result of the aging process can affect the level of sexual desire you feel (but it isn't usual to lose your sexual desire totally). High blood pressure sometimes interferes with sexual arousal, leading to impotence or lack of sexual response. However, many of the non-medically based sexual problems we have seen arise from the following actions, or lack of actions:

(1) *Not asking for what you want and not telling your partner what you don't want.* We have worked with countless couples who were dissatisfied with their sex lives for precisely this reason. Avoiding this problem is what the pleasure training session and the Mix 'n' Match Sexual Menu are all about. Let your partner know what you like and what you don't like. Letting him or her know *during* your sexual interactions provides an immediate opportunity to make adjustments.

(2) *Trying to force yourself to feel something you don't feel.* "When you're hot, you're hot and when you're not, you're not," as the popular saying goes. Trying to make yourself get an erection is one of the quickest ways to ensure impotence. The same is true for lubrication. The problem comes from deliberately trying to make something happen that is semi-automatic. If you get too self-conscious of the process, you interfere with it. It's like monitoring yourself when you can't go to sleep or can't urinate. The more you watch and try to make it happen, the worse it gets.

When one or both partners are trapped in the "performance" mode and therefore having trouble getting or staying aroused, most sex therapists, including us, follow a typical treatment pattern. We suggest that you start with pleasurable, sensual touching to help you connect with your natural sensuality and sexual excitement. Perhaps you could have a pleasure training session that did not involve breasts or genitals and then progress to full-body pleasure training sessions. The important principle here is to separate the pressure to perform (to have an orgasm or to have and maintain an erection) from the experience of being touched and aroused.

(3) *Not resolving unfinished business from the past.* Betrayal in your current or a previous relationship, experiences of sexual abuse or rape, or ingrained beliefs that sex is dirty or bad may seriously impede sexual functioning when not dealt with or addressed.

Sam and Betty had been married for twelve years. Sam was in the military and Betty was a homemaker. At the beginning of their relationship, before their children were born, they had sex three or four times a day. Around the time that they had their first child, Sam was on a tour of duty and gone for most of the year. When he returned, Betty became drastically turned off by sex and the resulting conflict eventually became the focus of their relationship.

As they talked over what had led to this deterioration, Betty told Sam that she felt used by him and had been angry with him ever since he had returned home. When he had come home from his long leave of absence, he had not talked to her, gotten reacquainted with her, or listened to her feelings about readjusting to his return—he just wanted to have sex as quickly as possible.

Betty and Sam attended our relationship class and decided to have a ceremony to help them leave that painful time behind. They also made an agreement that she could set the sexual pace if they were separated for any extended time again. Sam wrote a letter asking Betty to forgive him and Betty wrote a letter describing how much those events had upset her. They carried these letters with them for a week and then had a letter-burning ceremony, after which they went out for a celebration dinner.

After dealing with these issues, Sam and Betty were able to return to a more active sex life—not three times a day, but often once a day—which is a lot when you have kids!

(4) *Getting into sexual ruts and problem patterns.* The techniques that we have already suggested—using videotalk about sex, changing sexual patterns, and negotiating agreements about sexual interaction—can help you get out of sexual ruts and problem patterns.

Cheryl and Todd had been married for some years. Cheryl had progressively become non-orgasmic. It turned out that she was angry with Todd for frequently grabbing her breasts or sticking his hand down her pants in situations where she could not, or did not want to, respond. Todd agreed to make sure that any time he touched Cheryl outside the bedroom, he would not

include breasts and genitals or even innuendo statements. After a
couple of weeks of Todd's keeping his word about this, Cheryl
was ready to move to the pleasure training session.

The Tyranny of the "Big O" and Intercourse

We were supervising a marriage counselor in training when he
mentioned working with a couple who had stopped having sex
with each other. The husband had been on blood pressure medication for some time and therefore had not been able to get an erection. Bill asked, "Well, don't his fingers and tongue still work?"
Sex can involve much more than penis-vagina contact. We include
masturbation (self-stimulation), oral, and manual stimulation in our
definition of sex. If you limit yourself to intercourse, you may be
missing a lot and putting too much pressure on yourself or your
partner.

Some people have the idea that once they have a sexual partner,
they should no longer masturbate. In years past, there were many
pronouncements by scientific-sounding experts or admonitions by
nuns, priests and other religious types, telling us that masturbation
could cause blindness, hair on the palms, insanity, and so on. These
days, we know that masturbation does not do any of these terrible
things and, in fact, can enhance your sex life by teaching you what
you like and what arouses you. Bill can report the results of a
decades-long research project he has conducted that has proven
conclusively that masturbation does not cause hair to grow on the
palms or cause blindness. (When Bill says this, Pat is always quick to
point out that Bill *does* wear glasses, however.)

Masturbation can add to a relationship, not take away from it, as
long as one partner doesn't routinely masturbate and become disin-
terested in sexual interaction when the other partner wants sexual
contact. We also recommend that you don't masturbate so much
that you bleed or stop going to work. Masturbation can relieve

your partner of having to fulfill all your sexual needs and help you become more able to satisfy yourself so that you aren't at the whim of your partner's moods or preferences. The idea that two people are *always* going to be in sync sexually is a bit unrealistic.

Another idea that creates unrealistic expectations is the idea that when couples have sex, both must have orgasms (the "Big O") every time. Of course, if one of you is not achieving orgasm at all, this can be a concern, but occasionally one partner may not have an orgasm and still enjoy the sexual experience. Unhook yourself from the demand to have orgasms or to have your partner climax. If you relax and enjoy the process as one of sharing, pleasure, and connection, orgasm is likely to occur.

We have read books by experts that say that simultaneous orgasms are a myth and you shouldn't expect them in your sexual relationship. In our experience, with good communication, it *is* possible to synchronize orgasms (the results of another personal research project we have conducted). But again, the point is to remove the demand factor and focus on communicating what you like and don't like.

Am I Normal?

Because our culture has made sex seem weird and shameful, one of our goals is to "normalize" sex for you. When Pat was doing cotherapy with a couple for a sexual problem, her co-therapist said to the female client, "Why should your vagina be any different from your ear?" Of course, you will not get arrested for going out in public with your ear exposed. The point we're making is that most people treat sexual areas of the body as if they were disgraceful and not to be mentioned. Because sex is often not discussed openly, sometimes we all wonder if we are normal. Are my desires and sexual interests normal? Do other people have this problem or this worry? Is there something wrong with me? Are my genitals okay or is there something wrong with them? A sex therapist once gave a lecture to a boy's high school health class. He began his lecture with a startling statistic: "Ninety-five percent of all males masturbate," he told the boys. You could almost feel the silent sighs of relief from the anxious class members. After a pause the man continued, "and five percent lie." The laughter relieved any remaining tension. Once you discover that you are not alone or abnormal in your sexual feelings and practices, you can finally relax and accept yourself.

Bill did therapy with a man who initially sought help in reducing his high blood pressure. Alex also mentioned, casually, that maybe the high blood pressure was causing the impotence he had recently been experiencing. After several sessions, his blood pressure was lower and Alex was satisfied that it would remain so. Bill asked if there was anything else that concerned him. Alex nodded. He had felt too embarrassed at first to emphasize his concern about being impotent, but in truth, it was his main worry. Bill talked with him about the possibility of bringing his wife in for some joint sessions.

In the course of this discussion, Bill mentioned that impotence was a common occurrence for men. In fact, Bill himself had been impotent on occasion and had found that, the more he worried about it, the worse it got. Finally, Bill learned to relax and concentrate on enjoying himself sexually, rather than striving to get an erection. He had not had the problem for any length of time since then.

When Alex returned for the next session, he said that it was not necessary to have his wife come in because he no longer had a problem with impotence. When asked what had made the difference, he said that hearing that Bill had had the same problem made him feel it wasn't really irreversible and that his problem wasn't as unique as he had thought it was. When Bill happened to meet Alex and his wife several months later, she blushed and thanked Bill for the help he had given her husband, leaving Bill with the impression that things had continued in a positive direction.

Sexual Boredom

Couples commonly complain that they haven't been having sex frequently enough or that they are bored with their sex lives. It is easy for long-term married couples to fall into a pattern of doing sex the same old ways. We often prescribe the *Mix 'n' Match Sexual Menu* mentioned earlier; *changes in location* (moving from the bedroom to other rooms in the house or having sex in places outside the house); *changes in clothing* (many couples take off their clothes, get in bed and have sex—this is different from their courting patterns of taking off each other's clothes as part of the sexual foreplay; or we might suggest that they wear different clothes or costumes); or *reading or sharing erotic fantasies* with each other.

Fantasy Versus Action and Identity

Once a man came to see Bill for counseling. Arriving in a very agitated state, Jason announced desperately, "I'm a latent homosexual!" Bill, who as you may have guessed by now is not very keen on this sort of labeling, replied, "You are a latent many things: a latent dog, a latent president of the United States. What makes you think you'll become homosexual?" The man reported that lately, while having sex with his wife, he had been having fantasies of nude men. These fantasies had grown in intensity until they dominated his attention during sex with his wife. He feared he was on the road to becoming homosexual. Bill asked Jason if he wanted to pursue a homosexual lifestyle. He adamantly assured Bill that he was seeking help because he did not want to act on these fantasies, although deep down he feared he would. Bill said that if the man decided that he wanted help coming to terms with himself as homosexual, Bill would help him with that, but he had heard nothing to indicate that the man was homosexual.

Jason was amazed. "What about these fantasies?" he asked. Bill explained that there is a difference between fantasy and action and between fantasy and self-identity. Perhaps these fantasies were a message from deep inside about his real desires, but perhaps they were just random fantasies or natural curiosity. Bill said, "I bet these fantasies were infrequent at first and that the more you tried to get rid of them, the more intense and frequent they became." Jason agreed that this fit the facts. Bill recommended an experiment. Every time Jason started to make love with his wife, and even at random times during the day when he had a moment, he should try to make the nude men fantasies happen. A week of diligently practicing this exercise convinced Jason that the more he encouraged the fantasies, the less they ran the show.

This story illustrates two of our basic ideas. Your experience is just your experience and does not determine your identity; fantasies are fantasies and do not have to control your actions. If you have fantasies about being raped, it doesn't necessarily mean that you are "masochistic" (get pleasure from being hurt) or that you actually want to be raped. It just means that you have fantasies about being raped.

In the same way, your actions don't warrant a label. Your actions are your actions and your identity is your identity. While it has been helpful for some people to "come out of the closet" (publicly declare their homosexuality), for others making a firm decision or declaration about their sexual identity is a confusing, disempowering process. Labeling yourself sometimes closes down options. Research and many years of practice have shown us that many heterosexuals have had homosexual experiences in their lives and that many homosexuals have had heterosexual experiences. Doing is doing and being is being. Neither one has to determine the other.

A young man who was struggling to break free from his parents talked seriously about committing suicide. It took a few sessions for Mack to bring up his concerns; cautiously, he mentioned that he had always been attracted to men. When we explored this possibility, he finally acknowledged that he was gay. His suicidal thoughts and feelings left as soon as he came to this realization. Mack was able to tell some members of his family, which helped him feel that he was no longer hiding in shame. He also decided that there were some friends and family members who would not accept him as homosexual and that it was not crucial for him to tell everyone.

KEY POINTS: SEXUALITY

♥ Use the same principles of action complaints, action requests, meaningful praise, and negotiated agreements detailed earlier and apply them to sexual actions and interactions.

♥ It is normal to have fantasies and attractions. Just remember that you have choices about what you *do* about these fantasies and attractions. Be accountable for your actions and don't feel ashamed about your inner experience (fantasies, attractions, and preferences).

♥ Ask for what you want sexually, but don't demand it or force it on your partner. Don't shame your partner for asking for what he or she wants. Politely but firmly refuse to do something you are uncomfortable doing or don't want to do.

♥ Don't try to pretend or force yourself to be sexually excited when you are not, but also remember that doesn't mean you can't *do* sexual activities if you are not aroused.

ACTIONS STEPS: SEXUALITY

⇨ Ask your partner to tell you what he or she likes best about your sexual actions with him or her.

⇨ Tell your partner what you like best about his or her sexual actions with you.

⇨ Both of you fill out the Mix 'n' Match Sexual Menu and exchange it with each other.

⇨ Give each other pleasure training sessions. One partner focuses on stimulating the other, who reports what feels the best and what he or she would like more and less of.

7

LOVING YOUR PARTNER MORE THAN YOU LOVE YOUR STORIES

Verbs Don't Make a Whole Language

We have covered the basics of creating a loving relationship: acknowledging each person's feelings and perceptions in the relationship; using videotalk to communicate clearly, avoid misunderstandings, and negotiate agreements; and recognizing and changing problem patterns while preserving and expanding good patterns. In this chapter, we want to take you beyond this practical focus, to help you discover how to "stretch" yourself to make a relationship last and expand your ideas about what love is.

Are there times when the one you love makes your teeth itch with frustration because he is doing something that he knows you hate beyond reason? Because once again she is doing that thing you have asked her twenty times not to do? Do you sometimes think that you don't love your partner as much as you thought you did? Or do you feel that you have gotten so busy and distracted by your career or kids that you *might* love her if you knew who she was? Welcome to the real world of a long-term, intimate relationships. In a long-term relationship, your feelings of love will probably ebb and flow, even if you yearn for a constant steady stream. Fortunately, there are things you can do to *create* your feelings of love.

So far this book has focused on actions. There is more to love than actions, of course. It's just that actions provide the means for creating and communicating love. So we'll give you a few more action tips and then talk about other ways to create love—ways that don't involve *doing* anything but that come from changes you can make inside your heart.

We certainly don't claim to have all the answers about how to make relationships great. One of our favorite stories is the story about a guy who taught parenting classes. He was widely respected and acknowledged as an expert on helping parents deal with the challenges and joys of raising kids. He called the classes he taught *Ten Commandments for Parents*. They were really great classes and people flocked to them from all around. He was funny and clear and, even though he himself didn't have any children, parents learned a lot from his classes. Finally one day he met the woman of his dreams and they had a child together. He kept teaching the class, but after about a year he retitled it *Five Suggestions for Parents*. Then he and his wife were blessed with another child. He kept teaching but after another year he renamed the class *Three Tentative Hints for Parents*. After he and his wife had twins, he stopped teaching the class altogether.

When we were writing this book, we kept that story in mind. If these ideas help your relationship, use them. Remember, however, that this whole book is filled with *our* ideas about relationships. Don't turn our ideas and methods into more rules or beat each over the head with them. When we teach our relationship class, we often notice one partner turning to the other, poking him or her in the ribs with an elbow, and saying, "See, *you* do that." Seeing that discourages us, because it is the opposite of what we're advocating.

We are trying to point to some ways to help you decrease conflicts, validate rather than blame each other, and uncover and create love in your relationship. So *please* don't use these ideas as weapons. Use them as tools. *And if they don't work, don't use them.*

After working with hundreds of couples in marriage counseling for the past twenty years, we have discovered a few simple ideas that can help you rekindle the love that brought you together in the first place. We have heard people say, "I don't know if I ever really loved my husband/my wife." Trust us. The chances are, you did. Chances are, you still do but might only discover it after it is too late.

Here, in a nutshell, are the ways we have suggested in this book that you can create love.

(1) It is essential for each of you to be able to *acknowledge and validate* one another's feelings and points of view.

(2) After acknowledgment and validation come *actions*. Tell each other which actions you experience as loving and intimate and which actions don't work for you. If you run into a snag in action-land, negotiate until you can find some action that works for both of you.

(3) Next, *learn to recognize and change problem patterns of actions*. If you find yourself doing the same thing over and over again, but it doesn't work, get the message! Do something different. If you used to do things that worked better, then do those things again. This may seem obvious, but when you are in a rut, sometimes you can't see the obvious.

Hopefully you have gotten these three messages by now, so what we want to do now is take you a step further into the love zone—making love last a lifetime and stretching yourself beyond your current stories about love.

Making Love Last a Lifetime

We feel a little presumptuous discussing how to make a relationship last a lifetime, because we haven't been married for fifty years yet. But we have gathered hints from our own relationship and those we have come in contact with over the years. Whenever we meet a couple who has been married for years and still seems to have a great relationship, we ask the spouses how they have kept their love alive. What follows are our "Tentative Hints" for making love last a lifetime.

Are You a Relationship Wimp?

Early in our relationship, we came close to breaking up. Bill had made plans to visit his family in a nearby town. I became irritated when I realized that I could have gone with him if he had been willing to leave fifteen minutes later, but he went ahead and left without letting me know about it. We had already had arguments about Bill not including me in his plans, so this brought the sore subject up again.

When he returned home, I greeted Bill with my breakup speech, "Let's just forget this. It's too hard. I have all these kids; you've never been a parent before. I'm an only child; you come from a clan of eight children. Our religious backgrounds are different. It just seems like too much work. I can see that this relationship isn't going to work out. Let's just break up now before we get more attached."

Bill was not thrown off by my diatribe. He dealt with the immediate conflict over not including me in his social life by making an agreement to ask me if I wanted to be included in his plans in the future. When that issue was resolved, however, Bill asked me "Are you a relationship wimp?" "I'm not sure," I answered. "What is a relationship wimp?" Bill said, "I need to know that you won't wimp out on me. This conflict was relatively minor compared to the ones we'll have to deal with over the long haul. I'd like you to exercise your relationship muscle with these smaller conflicts so that it stays strong, in case something really tough comes up. That means not threatening to bail out or break up if we have a conflict. We may face illness, money problems, problems with kids—and I need to know you will stick it out *with* me."

A few months later, I turned the tables on Bill with this idea of being a relationship wimp. I could tell that Bill was down. When I asked him what the problem was, he said, "I don't like our lifestyle. I'm just not happy." After asking for some specifics (like what does a "lifestyle" look like), I confronted Bill about being a relationship wimp.

"If you are unhappy, I want to hear about it. Let's work on it together. I am a flexible person who could live in a cabin, in a condo, on a farm, or in town. I can change and adapt to new situations easily. What I want from you is the courage to create the relationship and lifestyle you want. I don't want to hear twenty years from now that you want a divorce because you never liked your lifestyle and thought I caused you to live a life you didn't want. It is up to you to demand that this be the life you want and hang in there with me while you're doing it. Even if I get upset by what you want, I'd like you to hang in there with me and work it out."

Bill says that that was the most important thing I have said to him so far, because it helped him to be true both to himself and to his commitment to our relationship. It's helped him speak up and stand his ground instead of wimping out by avoiding the conflict to keep the peace. That means that, if I get irritated because Bill refuses to work in the yard—he'd rather hire someone, while I thinks it's a waste of money—Bill is able to hang in there and argue it out until we come to a mutually satisfying resolution. Sticking up for what you want in a marriage without being hostile or dominating the other person can help your relationship survive in the long run.

Songwriter Joni Mitchell has a poignant line that expresses the idea that some people feel they have to leave relationships to find themselves again and get what they want: "In our possessive coupling, so much could not be expressed, so now I am returning to myself once again, those things that you and I suppressed." We don't think that you have to break up to find those "suppressed" areas of yourself. We think that, if you hang in there and stay committed to your dreams *and* your relationship, you can find a way to make it work.

We are making two points with our relationship wimp stories. First, stay through the tough times, even when you feel like leaving (in making this statement, we assume here that you are not being beaten and abused). There will most likely be times when you think, "Maybe this relationship was not such a hot idea after all." Second, take a loving, firm stance that you are not going to live a life you dislike, but at the same time, you are not going to toss out the relationship in search of some utopian marriage. This is it—no knights in shining armor or Playboy beauty queen fantasies. Stick with this one and turn it into your dream.

When Your Partner Is Ready to Leave

You may have bought this book because your partner is ready to give up on your relationship, but you are still in love with him or her and want to save the marriage. If you are in that situation, we have a couple of suggestions. First, do something unexpected but good for the relationship or for yourself. For example, if your spouse thinks you would never send flowers, send flowers. If your spouse sees you as dependent and thinks you would never take a trip by yourself, take a trip by yourself. The point is to surprise your discouraged spouse by showing him or her that you can change (which also implies, in a conveniently unstated way, that your spouse can change, too).

Second, we suggest you avoid the two extremes towards which people in your situation seem to gravitate. One is giving up easily on the relationship because your partner says he or she wants to end it—the old why-bother-to-fight syndrome. We have seen many marriages revived when they seemed over, so don't give up so easily. On the other hand, don't go to the extreme of becoming so desperate to save the relationship that your partner is turned off by your excessive dependency and subservience.

> *Jim and Gloria had been married for fifteen years. Jim had always seen Gloria as a strong-willed woman who usually got her way, so when she said she was thinking about getting a divorce, Jim just said, "Fine." For Gloria, Jim's reaction confirmed all her fears that he had never really loved her and did not care whether she left or not. They divorced with Gloria assuming that Jim was unscathed by their break-up. In fact, losing Gloria was devastating for Jim. It took him ten years to recover and love again. He had erred on the side of not telling Gloria how much he loved her and how unhappy he would be without her. While that would not have solved all of their problems, it might have affected Gloria, who had brought up divorce in part to see what reaction she would get. Jim's seemingly indifferent response ultimately sealed the fate of their relationship.*

From Jim and Gloria's story, you can see that giving up too easily is a bad idea. We have also seen just the opposite—being too desperate and pressuring your partner too much can result in repulsion.

> *Pat was working with Jeff and Sharon. Jeff was desperate to save the marriage, but Sharon wanted out. In a marriage counseling session, Jeff got down on his knees and tearfully pleaded with Sharon not to make him move out. Pat could see disgust in Sharon's eyes as she watched Jeff groveling on his knees, so she asked Sharon to leave the room for a minute. Alone with Jess, Pat said, "What you are doing is turning Sharon off. Try something else. While it is good to let her know that you still care,*

keep in mind that desperation is not sexy." Jeff listened to what
Pat had to say, but it was very hard for him to actually do what
she suggested. Ultimately, he was so driven by his feelings of loss
and abandonment that he drove Sharon away.

There was a time when Jeff stood a chance with Sharon, but he just couldn't live by the motto, "Desperation is not sexy." He should have kept more of his feelings to himself. It was okay for him to feel desperate, but the way in which he expressed those feelings alienated his partner. Jim, on the other hand, might have saved his marriage if he had been willing to show more of his feelings to his partner.

Report from a Long-term Relationship

Pat and I conduct real-life research to find out how couples stay together happily for life. I was invited to attend a party for a couple who was celebrating their fiftieth wedding anniversary. The couple seemed to have a lot of fun together and their relationship was lively and playful. I didn't know the couple but had come with a friend. As the evening progressed, I found myself seated on the couch next to the wife. I told her that I was a marriage counselor, curious about how people kept their relationships thriving over the long-term, as she and her husband had done.

She said, "I was married to five men." I was shocked. "You mean you had *four* other husbands before him?!"

Laughing, she answered, "No, he always had the same name— it's just that he was five different people inside. When I first fell in love with him, he was a handsome young man full of ambition and fun. I fell in love with that man. Then he became a workaholic. I didn't like the workaholic so much at first, but eventually I learned to fall in love with that man, too. Then he went through what you young folks call a mid-life crisis. That was a tough time, but I eventually fell in love with that husband too. Then he retired and at first was kind of lost, but he finally found his way. I learned to love that man too. *Now* look at him. He is an old man with baggy skin hanging from his arms. That's not the handsome young man I married! But even though that was not the man I fell in love with, I have fallen in love with this one, too. That's the secret. I learned to love my five husbands."

Change is inevitable. Learning to love your partner through those changes, discovering the new person he or she has come to be, is one of the ways to make your relationship last.

Wind-up Toys and Bowls

We have heard people say that relationships are always hard work. That may overstate the case. Bill and I each have our own relationship analogies. I think that relationships are like wind-up toys. Sometimes you have to pick them up and re-wind them, but most of the time you can just enjoy them. There may be months or even years during which you are having to spend much of your time winding up your relationship—particularly when you are going through major changes like having a baby, moving, mourning the loss of family members, or having that baby grow up and leave. But, assuming the spring in your wind-up toy doesn't break, most of the time you can just enjoy your relationship. What we have covered so far in this book is how to wind the spring just tight enough to be able to enjoy your relationship for a while.

While I think of the wind-up toy, Bill thinks of the relationship as a bowl. (I thought that was unusual for a man who has spent so little time in the kitchen.) For Bill, the bowl represents commitment to the relationship. When you first get to know someone and you don't feel much commitment, your bowl is pretty small. If the person forgets a lunch date a couple of times or is rude to you, the bowl overflows with the conflict and the relationship is over. However, if you decide to stick with the relationship, your bowl gets a little bigger in order to contain the disappointments and problems.

You start to date someone and you have your first argument. Do you end the relationship or stick with it? You've been married for some time and discover your partner has been unfaithful. Does this transgression overflow the bowl or can the bowl contain it? If you stick around through whatever happens, you've got a pretty big bowl. We're not talking about being a victim or just accepting whatever the other person dishes out. That's not commitment— that's being a doormat!

Bill has a friendship that illustrates this point.

My friend Michael moved to Seattle. I wrote him five times in the first year after he had moved and got no reply to any of the letters. Finally, I got Michael's telephone number from directory assistance, called him, and hassled him for not staying in touch. With most acquaintances, I wouldn't have bothered, but I was committed to maintaining my friendship with Michael. My bowl for this relationship was big.

Pat's Four Principles

After my first marriage of sixteen years ended, I did a lot of thinking about what makes relationships last. I thought about couples who succeed in weathering crises and those who throw in the towel. I concluded that four qualities/abilities are crucial to make relationships last: commitment, skills, integrity, and humor.

Commitment is defined as the state of being *dedicated* emotionally and intellectually to some action. When we looked in the dictionary we were thrilled to find that the definition included *action*. You may commit in your mind and your heart, but you must express that commitment through actions.

The preceding six chapters of this book have focused on skills. We can teach you to communicate and negotiate easily enough. What is hard to teach, but we think essential to having a relationship last, is integrity. You will have a hard time staying in a relationship with someone who lies to you, cheats on you, or deceives you. When our daughter Angie was in college, Pat asked Angie what she was looking for in a husband. Angie said that integrity was highest on her list. We were happy that she had learned that, because we have seen so much pain caused by the lack of integrity in spouses. (We have also seen spouses realize their lack of integrity and change.) When you don't know whether or not your husband has paid the bills he said he would pay or whether or not your wife was really working late or being unfaithful, it becomes very challenging to keep enlarging that bowl or winding up that toy.

How can you stick with a partner who is always grim and serious? Life's too short to be taken too seriously. Many conflicts can be resolved by laughing with each other rather than convening an earnest discussion. We consider laughter to be the mental-health test for our relationship. If we aren't having an occasional laugh together, then we need to do something to lighten up!

Next we'll give you some ideas about how to create the experience of more love in you and your partner.

KEY POINTS: MAKING RELATIONSHIPS LAST

♥ Stay through the changes, even though your impulse is to leave.

♥ Let your partner know how much you care in a non-smothering way.

♥ Don't be a relationship wimp—don't withdraw from the relationship or threaten to leave when there is conflict. Commit to creating a great relationship for both you and your partner.

♥ Learn to use integrity, commitment, skills, and humor to carry you through.

ACTION STEPS: MAKING RELATIONSHIPS LAST

⇨ If you feel like leaving the relationship, postpone it, unless you are in danger.

⇨ Talk to your partner about something you've wanted but feel you have to give up because of your relationship. Find out if there is a way that you can get some part of what you want in a way that supports your relationship.

When You're Not Sure You Are in Love Anymore

One of the most important things we have learned in the last twenty years is that you don't have to have the feelings *before* you take action. You can simply plunge ahead and change what you do and, often, your feelings will follow. For example, you may not *feel* assertive, but once you start doing assertive actions, sure enough, you begin to feel more assertive. The same is true for love.

You may wonder, "Do I really love my spouse?" Instead of pondering this difficult question, why not try taking action? What would you do tonight if the person next to you in bed was the love of your life? Would you hold her in a certain way? Would you say certain things to him? Over and over again we have observed that once people start to *do* loving actions, they find themselves *feeling* more loving. Even if things are going well in your relationship, why not stretch just a little further by doing a few more things that you would do if your partner were your true love. Some people say, "But I don't want to lie." We're not suggesting that you lie, only that you act *as if*. Don't say, "I love you," if you don't know whether you love your partner. But you could do loving actions just as an experiment. It would not be a lie to hold your partner, kiss him, or ask her about how her day was.

Perhaps there are things you can do to remind yourself to act in loving ways, such as writing a note to yourself in your organizer, putting a stick-up note on your mirror, or leaving a reminder in the car. Whatever ways you remember appointments or other important dates, use the same techniques to remind yourself to act in loving ways.

Most couples start out feeling in love. It is as if there is a golden light of love shining between them. Then layers and layers of duties and experiences methodically cover and dim the light. Kids come along, mortgages are taken on, there are bills to pay, and arguments and disappointments happen. Pretty soon you can't even see the light and you begin to wonder if it has gone out entirely. We have offered some skills for you to use to clear away the debris and find out if there is still a golden light of love underneath it all. In our experience, most of the time couples find that the light is still shining once they have cleared away their problem patterns.

Don't Wait

It is easy to slip into the habit of waiting for something to happen first, before you start being more loving. Are you thinking that you could finally love your partner if only he would change something . . . get over his last relationship . . . be less co-dependent . . . hold a job . . . take your side against his parents . . . or start sharing his feelings? If you didn't wait for anything to happen first—if you just loved your partner now—what might be possible? We urge you *not* to wait. Love your partner now even if the conditions are less than ideal.

Before Pat and I got married, I owned a car jointly with my friend Michael. It was a used car and required ongoing care to keep it running. After a while we noticed that the car was breaking down often, usually from things that could have been prevented if minor maintenance chores had been done on time. When we sat down together to talk about the problem, we discovered that each of us had a 50/50 mindset: "I've done my part; now it's his turn to check the oil or fill the water in the battery." The problem was that, whenever one of us failed to do his 50 percent—even if he did 49 percent—maintenance that needed to be done slipped through the cracks. What we ended up with was a broken-down car more often than we wanted. So we came up with a plan. Each of us would take 100 percent responsibility for the car and not count on the other to do any of the ongoing maintenance checks. That way, if either one of us procrastinated or fell behind on his part, the car would still be maintained. It may sound crazy, but what we got was a car that worked!

The same principles apply to relationships. Sometimes people hold back, waiting for the other person to carry his or her half of the relationship. In the meantime, things fall between the cracks. Problems get swept under the rug. *I approached him last time after an argument, so it's his turn this time.* That's 50/50 thinking. You get to feel justified with that kind of thinking, but in all likelihood your relationship will break down eventually. If you each take 100 percent responsibility for maintaining the relationship, you will most likely reap the rewards of a relationship that works.

Creating a Context for Love

We have seen people give up on their relationships because they believed that it's impossible to make someone love you. That is not entirely true. Pat's dad used to say that it was a simple fact of life that to get love, you have to act lovable. If you act in a way that invites love, then you are likely to be loved.

When Pat and I were first together, I described to Pat what I thought wonderful relationship would be. Pat was a fast learner and quickly figured out what actions would create the context in which my love would grow. These were all things Pat usually did anyway, such as touching freely, refraining from criticism, and being supportive.

It's usually effortless to do loving actions while the first blush of lust and love is still in the air, but if the blush has paled, you can still take actions you could do that would be likely to create love. You probably know the things that *don't* work: criticizing, complaining, avoiding, withdrawing, attacking. You also probably know the things that create fertile ground for love to take root: praise, appreciation, touching, honesty, consideration, acceptance. Perhaps your partner can be even more specific in identifying the conditions for his or her love garden.

Don't Fall in Love with Your Ideas

We have focused on showing you how to teach your partner what love is for you and how to elicit preferences and definitions of love from him or her. But what if your partner never really gives your kind of love? Is it still possible to receive love from him or her? Perhaps he is giving love to you in the only way he is able. Perhaps she is giving love to you in the only way she has ever experienced it. Bill tells a beautiful story that illustrates our point.

While I was growing up, my father would often slip me a five dollar bill and say, "Here's five dollars—don't tell your mom." My mom thought that my father was too generous with money. As I thought about this later in life, when my father was diagnosed with cancer, I realized that this was his way of saying, "I love you." I, like most people, preferred to get my love directly with the words "I love you" and a hug. But I also realized that this was my father's way of expressing his love. So, every time my father slipped me some money (he never broke this habit) and said, "Don't tell your mother," I would mentally translate that into, "I love you, son."

When my father first became ill with cancer, I called him on the phone. When the conversation came to a close, I said, "I just want you to know how much I appreciate all you've done for me as a father. I love you, Dad." My father replied, dismissively, "Yeah, I love all my kids." I just shrugged and again realized my father's discomfort with any direct expressions of love.

In the third and final year of my father's fight with cancer, he came to stay in Arizona where I was going to college, but after a short time he became so ill that he had to return to Nebraska. As I was sitting with him in the departure lounge at the airport, we both knew that this was probably the last time we would see each other. I turned to him and said, "I love you, Dad." My father looked away and said, "Well, I love all you kids." While I looked into my father's eyes, I repeated very slowly, "No, Dad, I want to make sure you hear me. *I love you.*" My father started to cry, we hugged, and he whispered, "I love you."

My father finally acted in accord with my map of love; yet, even if he had never said, "I love you," I still would have known that he loved me. I understood that "Here's five dollars—don't tell your mom" was love, too.

This story has two morals. The first: realize that your partner may be giving love in the only way he or she can. The second: sometimes people can be taught to express love in different ways— ways that more closely resemble their partner's map. So keep telling your partner in a loving way what you want and maybe he or she will eventually learn to do it "your way." We're suggesting that you consider the idea that *what your partner is doing now could be love, even if it doesn't look like love to you.*

Dan and Liz came to see Pat. As soon as they sat down, Dan stated that he was very committed to the marriage and wanted it to last. When Pat asked Liz for her goal in therapy, she said that she wanted her freedom. After some discussion, it became clear that freedom had something to do with spending time with her friends, so Pat asked (unpacking that packaged word freedom), "How would freedom look in the context of this marriage? Would it be one night a week out with your friends?" Liz said, "No. One night a month out with my friends. He can pick the friends and I won't go to a bar."

Pat was thinking, This is going to be a piece of cake, *when she* asked Dan, *"So if Liz goes out one night a month, you pick the friends, and she doesn't go to a bar, can you be supportive of her going out and pleasant to her when she comes home?"* To Pat's surprise Dan said, *"Absolutely not! It violates everything I believe about marriage."* The packaged word, *marriage,* for Dan meant that every minute that the two of them were not at work, they were to be together. While this was not close to Pat's definition of marriage—it was more her idea of suffocation—but she was willing to help them negotiate. Dan would not compromise.

They eventually separated and Liz found out what freedom truly entailed. As the divorce process began, Dan returned alone to Pat's office. Sadly, he said, *"I would do anything to have Liz back. I realize how wrong I was. I now can see that I loved my ideas more than I love my wife."*

If you find yourself getting upset about something in your relationship, be sure that you are not more devoted to your ideas or stories about love than you are to the flesh-and-blood human being before you.

Who's Got the Remote Control Now?

After receiving a brochure inviting him to attend one of our relationship classes, one of Pat's former clients sent back a note saying that he would like to attend, but that right now love was merely a dangling participle for him. While we thought that was very funny, it also showed what many people feel: that love is something that is either in their lives or it isn't, and that they have little power to create it.

Remember how you felt when you were first in love? You glowed. You were filled with love and you projected that loving energy out into the world. Friends could tell there was something different about you. It was as if love had turned on all the lights and thrown open all the doors and windows in your inner house. If someone cut you off while you were driving, you didn't curse or make rude gestures. You were in love. All was right with the world. No one and nothing could impinge on that feeling. No one could turn off your lights or close those doors and windows.

Then after a while, you closed a window here and a door there. A little less light was thrown out into the world. Daily life went on, with its distractions and hurts. You shut off a few more lights to conserve energy and closed a few more doors. In time, the house began to feel dark and cold, as if the lights had gone out entirely and the doors and windows were boarded up tight. Disillusioned with your relationship, you wondered why you didn't feel that love anymore. You used to light up at the sight of your partner; now maybe you're annoyed or bored. At times like this, you may start to think about finding someone new—someone who could turn on those lights again and get you to open the doors and windows. You begin searching for what we think of as the holder of the remote control, waiting for someone to come along who has the magic device that will turn you on once again. But you are forgetting that it is *your* house. *You* can throw open your doors and windows and turn on all your lights from the inside any time you want. You can decide that you are going to give up your search for the holder of remote control and let that love come from you—inside out. Rather than waiting for someone to bring love to you, you begin to act from love.

The Land of Warm Fuzzies

We know a story that makes the point we want to end with. It may sound kind of corny, but indulge us.

Once there was a land in which everyone was happy and healthy. Love was everywhere. The reason for all this wonderfulness was that everyone had an appendage that grew on the side of the body, a bag of skin that contained warm fuzzies. Warm fuzzies are little balls that feel like day-old chicks, all soft and fuzzy. When you give one to someone, it sort of melts into them. When you first put it on them, it feels warm and nice, and as it sinks in, it feels like love and validation. People in this land routinely went around giving each other warm fuzzies, so naturally everyone felt happy and healthy and loved.

One day, however, a witch came to the land, hawking her potions and medicines to cure any ailment. Since nobody got sick or unhappy in this land, she couldn't sell anything. She was just about to pack up and move on when she came up with a scheme. She sidled up to the first person she saw who was giving away a warm fuzzy and whispered in his ear, "Hey, you shouldn't be giving those away like there's no tomorrow. I just moved here and in the land I came from, there was a virus that infected the warm fuzzies and caused a severe shortage of them." The man thought about that after she left and got a bit worried. *Just to be on the safe side,* he thought, *maybe I'd better save my warm fuzzies for my family. Nobody will notice the difference.*

What he didn't realize was that, like any other part of the body, the warm fuzzy part atrophied if it wasn't used. The more he kept his warm fuzzies to himself, the fewer his body made, until one day he reached in to what had always been a full pouch and found only two warm fuzzies left. He became convinced that the warm-fuzzy-attacking virus had arrived in the land and started helping the witch spread the rumor.

Soon, everyone was hoarding their warm fuzzies and finding fewer and fewer of them in their pouches. People were getting sick with all sorts of new ailments; worse, everybody was feeling very lonely, unworthy, and unloved. The witch was doing a bang-up business. She even opened a store that sold cold pricklies, which looked like warm fuzzies, but were made of fake fur. When you put one on someone, as if you were giving them a *real* warm fuzzy, they felt okay when they first received the bogus substitute, but as it was absorbed, it left them feeling empty and bleak. Things were terrible in Warm-Fuzzy Land.

One day a strange woman arrived in town who had a big bag full of warm fuzzies, which she gave away to anyone and everyone. People tried to warn her about the virus, but she ignored their warnings. After several weeks, others could see that she still had an overflowing bag of warm fuzzies. They became curious. *"Don't you see,"* she implored, *"the more you give away, the more you get."* It sounded crazy and illogical, but she made a few converts, and soon their warm fuzzy bags were also overflowing. The rumor was dispelled and people went back to their previous pattern of generosity. The witch was forced to close her shops and move on.

That's the secret, of course. The more love you give, the more you *have* to give. We hope this book has contributed to your sense of love and helped you come from a place of love within yourself. If it has, please spread it around. God knows this world could use a bit more love.

KEY POINTS: LOVE

♥ Get out of 50/50 thinking. Take 100 percent responsibility for your relationship. Don't wait for your partner to do his or her half first.

♥ Expand your story about what love is to include what your partner does. Consider that what your spouse is doing right now may be his or her way of showing love.

♥ Rather than looking for love, come from a place of love within yourself. You have the power to let your love shine, rather than waiting for someone else to throw the switch.

ACTIONS STEPS: LOVE

⇨ Create the setting for love to grow. When you go home tonight, act as if the person you are with is the love of your life. Imagine the voice tones you would use, how you would touch him or her, what you would say—then let all your actions emanate love.

⇨ Commit yourself to acting loving on a daily basis. Put up reminder notes at your office and on your bathroom mirror to remind yourself that you are taking responsibility for creating more love in your relationship.

Index